The People of
EDINBURGH
and
LEITH
at Home and Abroad

1800-1850

By
David Dobson

CLEARFIELD

Copyright © 2022
by David Dobson
All Rights Reserved

Published for Clearfield Company by
Genealogical Publishing Company
Baltimore, Maryland
2022

ISBN: 9780806359533

INTRODUCTION

The second half of the eighteenth century saw the construction of the New Town of Edinburgh, to the north of the medieval burgh and across the Nor' Loch. Simultaneously the Scottish Enlightenment gave Edinburgh much of its international renown. Edinburgh became the capital of the Scottish professional classes, the surgeons, the physicians, the lawyers, and the architects. It was also the centre of publishing, banking, the Church, and insurance companies, as well as distinguished educational establishments. The New Town of Edinburgh was further embellished through the erection of the Observatory, Calton Hill monuments, National Gallery of Scotland, Register House, and the Royal Bank of Scotland. Transportation improvements, such as the Leith Docks, introduction of the railways, and construction of the George IV Bridge and other bridges within the city, enabled Edinburgh to expand. During the 19th century, the affluent would abandon the Old Town in favour of the New Town, the middle classes and the skilled workers moved out to the suburbs, while those who had no option remained in the Old Town.

During the first half of the 19th century, Edinburgh and Leith remained as two distinct communities. Leith only became a burgh in 1833 and remained so until it was formally integrated into Edinburgh in 1922. Leith functioned as the port of Edinburgh; the import-export trade initially was confined to western Europe but eventually became worldwide. Timber was imported from Scandinavia, grain from the Baltic and wine from France and Spain, while coal from nearby coalfields was shipped to Scandinavia and the Netherlands. Leith was famous for its glass and bottle-making works, brewing, distilling, and warehousing. Leith was also an important shipbuilding centre; for example, the S.S.Sirius, built in Leith in 1837, was the first steamship to cross the Atlantic. Many immigrant transports sailed from Leith, including the William Young of Leith bound for Australia in 1828, or the Symmetry bound for Argentina in 1825, or the Jean from Leith bound for Quebec in 1828.

This book is largely based on monumental inscriptions in and around Edinburgh, contemporary newspapers and magazines, together with a host of sources found in archives. The entries combine information on people who went abroad as well as those who remained in Edinburgh.

A list of References begins on page 161.

David Dobson
Dundee, 2022

Queen's Park, Edinburgh. Review of Scottish Volunteers, August 7, 1860

Head of 'West Bow, Edinburgh

"Freemen of Edinburgh Trades" by Roderick Chalmers. The trades shown include a wright, a painter, a cooper, a slate mason, a glazier, a plumber and a bower. They are shown in the working dress of their professions, with a background of Holyroodhouse. The painter alone is shown as a gentleman, seated and wearing a periwig [far right].

Street scene, Edinburgh

PEOPLE OF EDINBURGH & LEITH, AT HOME AND ABROAD, 1800-1850

ABERCROMBIE, DAVID, a printer, son of Alexander Abercromby a grocer and burgess, was admitted as a burgess of Edinburgh on 27 March 1812. [EBR]

ABERCROMBIE, JOHN, a surgeon, was admitted as a burgess of Edinburgh on 31 October 1804. [EBR]

ABERNETHY, ALEXANDER, a candlemaker, a former apprentice to John Kedie a candlemaker burgess, was admitted as a burgess of Edinburgh on 22 June 1807. [EBR]

ADAM, ALEXANDER, a tailor, former apprentice to Andrew Adam a tailor, was admitted as a burgess of Edinburgh On 14 August 1810. [EBR]

ADAM, ELIZABETH, born 1820, wife of Rowand Ronald, died in Sydney, New South Wales, Australia, on 23 October 1847. [St Cuthbert's gravestone, Edinburgh]

ADAM, JOHN SHEDDEN, born 1823, died in Wahroonga, Sydney, New South Wales, Australia, on 5 December 1906. [St Cuthbert's gravestone, Edinburgh]

ADAMS, RICHARD, born 1793, an architect, with his wife Anna and four children, emigrated via Leith on the Symmetry bound for Argentina on 22 May 1825. [SRP.18]

ADAMSON, WILLIAM MACPHIE, a fish curer and cooper in Leith, was admitted as a burgess of Edinburgh on 27 June 1838, having married Euphemia Stewart, daughter of James Stewart a silversmith burgess, [EBR]; later in 51 Giles Street, Leith, 1849. [POD]

ADIE, ALEXANDER JAMES, born 1774, an optician, died on 4 December 1858., husband of Marion ......, born 1783, died on 26 April 1865. [Greyfriars gravestone]

AIKMAN, GEORGE, an engraver, 29 North Bridge, Edinburgh, 1849. [POD]

AIKMAN, JAMES, born 1801, a leather merchant in Edinburgh, died on 26 January 1848, his wife Anne Sutherland, born 1801, died on 4 November 1883. [St Cuthbert's gravestone, Edinburgh]

AIKMAN, JAMES, son of James Aikman in High Street, Edinburgh, died in Charleston, South Carolina, on 20 February 1841. [EEC.20192]

AIKMAN, JOHN, born 1770, founder of the Congregational churches in Scotland, pastor of Argyle Square chapel in Edinburgh, died on 6 February 1834. [Greyfriars gravestone]

AIKMAN, MARY BROWN, daughter of George Aikman an engraver in Edinburgh, married J. Gray from Canada West, in New York in 21 March 1853. [EEC.22416]

AIKMAN, PETER, born 1819, second son of George Aikman, an engraver, [1788-1805], and his wife Alison Mackay, [1791-1844], died in New York on 15 September 1883. [St Cuthbert's gravestone, Edinburgh]

AIMERS, S., tailor, 38 Rankeillor Street, Edinburgh, 1849. [POD]

AIRD, JAMES, born 1797, a carpenter, with his wife Mary, and a child, emigrated from Leith aboard the <u>Symmetry</u> bound for Buenos Ayres, Argentina, on 22 May 1825, landed there on 11 August 1825. [SRP.18]

AIRE, CECIL, youngest daughter of Lieutenant John Aire of the Royal Navy, died in Wellington Place, Leith, on 30 November 1825. [NRS]

AIRE, JAMES RITCHIE, born 1792 in Leith, son of Lieutenant John Aire and his wife Christian Ritchie, a Brevet Captain of the 64th Native Infantry of the Bengal Army, a soldier from 1808 until 1827. [BA]

AITCHISON, JAMES, son of William Aitchison a brewer in Edinburgh, in Tilbury, Lower Canada, and later in London, Upper Canada, fled to the USA to avoid imprisonment, letters, 1831-1838. [NRS.GD1.92.18]

AITCHISON, WILLIAM ALEXANDER, born 20 March 1834, son of Archibald Aitchison and his wife Ann Ferguson Jamieson, a Lieutenant of the 59th Regiment of Virginia Volunteers, of the Army of the Confederate States, died in Richmond, Virginia, on 26 January 1865. [St Cuthbert's gravestone, Edinburgh]

AITKEN, GEORGE, in St Croix, Danish West Indies, subscribed to a deed in Edinburgh on 9 June 1795. [NRS.RD5.92.723]

AITKEN, JAMES, a farrier, 14 Potterrow, Edinburgh, 1849. [POD]

AITKEN, JOHN GEORGE, son of John Aitken a physician in Edinburgh, died in Demerara on 3 August 1803. [DPCA.73]

ALEXANDER, ARTHUR, born 18 August 1812 in Ceylon, the Deputy Inspector of Hospitals, died on 10 April 1883. [St Cuthbert's gravestone, Edinburgh]

ALEXANDER, RICHARD, from Edinburgh, father of John Thomson Alexander, an infant who died in Park Lane, Toronto, Ontario, on 6 September 1855. [EEC.788794]

ALEXANDER, ROBERT, elder of South Leith parish in 1825. [SLR]

ALISON, ARCHIBALD, born in 1758, minister of St Paul's, died in 1839, husband of Dorothy Gregory, born in 1754, died in 1830. [St John's gravestone, Edinburgh]

ALISON, Dr CHARLES, surgeon aboard HMS Endymion, son of James Alison in Edinburgh, died at the Cape of Good Hope on 28 March 1843. [EEC.20614]

ALISON, JAMES, in Leith, applied to settle in Canada on 1 March 1815. [NRS.RH9]

ALISON, ROBERT, son of Robert Alison a workman in Nether Liberton, was apprenticed to Alexander Grieve, a bookbinder in Edinburgh, for six years on 11 May 1797. [ERA]

ALISON, WILLIAM, in Leith, applied to settle in Canada on 1 March 1815. [NRS.RH9]

ALLAN, ANDREW SIMPSON, son of James of Redford, was indentured to David Allan, a plumber in Edinburgh, for six years, on 10 June 1790. [ERA]

ALLAN, GEORGE, nephew of Alexander Allan an Episcopalian minister in Edinburgh, died in St Croix, Danish West Indies, in April 1820. [SM]; he subscribed to a deed in St Croix on 24 June 1819 in which he referred to Reverend Alexander Allan and his cousin's children. [NRS.RD5.168.283]

ALLAN, ISABELLA, daughter of Thomas Allan a merchant in Leith, married Peter Cleghorn, a barrister at law, in Madras, India, on 20 July 1819. [SM.85]

ALLAN, JAMES GLEN, born 1815, died in Nova Scotia, on 12 January 1886. [Old Calton gravestone, Edinburgh]

ALLAN, JAMES C., from Leith, married Janet Campbell McKenzie, eldest daughter of John McKenzie in Urquhart, in Geelong, Australia, on 15 January 1858. [CM.21367]

ALLAN, JOHN, born 3 January 1747 in Edinburgh Castle, the eldest son of William Allan and his wife Isabel Maxwell, the family emigrated to Nova Scotia around 1750, he married Mary Patton on 10 October 1767, a politician and public official, died at Lubeck, Maine, on 7 February 1805. [DCB]

ALLAN, JOHN, from Edinburgh, was naturalised in Charleston, South Carolina, by the Court of Admiralty on 29 November 1797. [NARA.M1183.1]

ALLAN, JOHN, son of James Allan, a writer, was apprenticed to Inglis and Dewar, surgeons in Edinburgh, for five years on 16 May 1799. [ERA]

ALLAN, JOHN, born in Edinburgh before 1815, son of Francis Allan and his wife Isabella Sheach, died in Peru. [Old Calton gravestone, Edinburgh]

ALLAN, ROBERT, a surgeon in Edinburgh, versus his wife Anna Scott, a Process of Divorce in 1817. [NRS.CC8.5.36]

ALLAN, THOMAS, a merchant in Leith, 1795-1797. [NRS.CS96.1207]

ALLAN, WILLIAM, a shipmaster in Leith, testament, 1807, Comm. Edinburgh. [NRS]

ALSTEIN, FREDERICK A. M., born 1815, died in Demerara on 9 March 1860. [Dean gravestone, Edinburgh]

ALSTEIN, FREDERICK ROBERT, born 1842, son of Frederick A. M. Alstein and his wife Janet, died in Demerara on 13 March 1866. [Dean gravestone, Edinburgh]

ALSTON, DAVID, son of Gavin Alston, a printer, was apprenticed to Innes and Wallace, gunsmiths in Edinburgh, for seven years on 5 October 1797. [ERA]

ALSTON, J., a grocer and spirit dealer, 50 Tolbooth Wynd, Leith, 1849. [POD]

ALVES, JOHN, from Edinburgh, died in Kingston, Jamaica, on 14 December 1825. [S.637.104]

AMOS, A., a corn merchant in Echo Bank, Edinburgh, 1849. [POD]

AMOS, MARGARET, born 1812, daughter of Andrew Amos, [1775-1855], and his wife Jane Oliver, [1781-1832], died in Troy, USA, on 2 October 1837. [Liberton gravestone]

ANDERSON, ALEXANDER, Deacon of the Masons of South Leith, a letter, 1829. [SLR]

ANDERSON, ANDREW, son of James Anderson in New York, and Mary Anderson or Watt, the daughter of John Watt a merchant in Edinburgh, a deed dated Brussels in 1817. [NRS.RD5.219.273] [Greyfriars gravestone]

ANDERSON, DAVID, born 1775, a farmer, with his wife Mary and two children, emigrated via Leith on the Symmetry bound for Argentina on 22 May 1825. [SRP.18]

ANDERSON, HENRY, a cordiner burgess of Edinburgh, father of Robert Anderson, a merchant in Antigua, who was admitted as a burgess of Edinburgh in 1812. [EBR]

ANDERSON, JAMES, from Leith, a merchant in Virginia, a sasine, 1791. [NRS.RS.Caithness.211]; in America in 1795. [NRS.CS17.14,140]

ANDERSON, Dr JAMES, a Fellow of the Royal College of Surgeons of Edinburgh, died in Port-of-Spain, Trinidad, on 30 September 1826. [BM.21.119]

ANDERSON, JAMES, a surgeon in Trinidad, subscribed to a deed there which referred to Thomas Young a physician in Edinburgh, and his wife Barbara Gibson, to James Hay a physician in Edinburgh, to James Hutton a physician in Edinburgh, to Robert Young an upholsterer in Edinburgh, deed written by Robert Young Anderson, a writer in Edinburgh, 1815. [NRS.RD5.73.29]

ANDERSON, JAMES, late of the Scottish Insurance Company in Edinburgh, died in Montreal, Quebec, on 13 May 1833. [AJ.4460]

ANDERSON, JAMES, a teacher in Edinburgh, father of James Anderson, a physician in Mebourne, Australia, 1856. [NRS.S/H]

ANDERSON, JOHN, a merchant in Leith, heir to his brother James Anderson, a merchant in Virginia, 1790. [NRS.S/H]; a sasine, Caithness, 1791. [NRS.RS.Caithness.21]

ANDERSON, JOHN, a merchant in Leith, father of William Anderson in Augustura, Guayana Province, Venezuela, a deed, 1819. [NRS.RD5.166.130]

ANDERSON, JOHN, from Edinburgh, father of a daughter who was born in New York on 13 January 1839. [SG.8.742]

ANDERSON, JOHN IZATT, born 1834, died in New Zealand on 10 October 1866. [Greyfriars gravestone]

ANDERSON, MARY STUART, second daughter of James Anderson in Burrowloch, married Samuel Darwick Beresford, MD, from Berbice, in Edinburgh on 7 January 1830. [BM.27.549]

ANDERSON, P., married Mary McLean, eldest daughter of John McLean of Kingston, Jamaica, in Edinburgh on 16 November 1827. [S.821.744]

ANDERSON, ROBERT BRUNTON, MD, born 1820, died in Jamaica on 5 December 1842. [Dean gravestone]

ANDERSON, WILLIAM, a gardener in Edinburgh, applied to settle in Canada on 8 March 1815.]NRS.RH9]; bound via Greenock for Canada in 1815. [TNA.CO385.2]

ANDERSON, WILLIAM, in Barbados, eldest son of the late John Anderson a merchant in Leith, subscribed to a deed in Venezuela on 9 June 1819, which appointed John Buchan Brodie, a Writer to the Signet, in Edinburgh, as his attorney. [NRS.RD5.166.130]

ANDERSON, WILLIAM, in Dominica, eldest son and heir of William Anderson in London, appointed Thomas Baillie, Solicitor to the Supreme Court in Edinburgh, as his attorney, deed written by James

Sword, apprentice to Thomas Baillie, subscribed in New York in 1821. [NRS.RD5.213.521][also see RD5.215.579]

ANDERSON, WILLIAM, an elder of South Leith parish on 1 October 1843. [SLR]

ANDREW, JOHN, son of John Andrew a merchant in Edinburgh, died in Jamaica on 25 April 1817. [S.31.17]

ANDREWS, PETER, in Leith, father of David Andrews, born 1854, died in Chile in 1882. [S.12081]

ANGUS, ALAN, garrison schoolmaster in Edinburgh Castle, versus his wife Mary Jamison, married in 1810, divorced in 1816. [NRS.CC8.5.37]

ANGUS, ROBERT, a haberdasher, 68 Tolbooth Wynd, Leith, 1849. [POD]

ANNAN, JAMES, a plasterer, Bread Street, Edinburgh, 1849. [POD]

ARBUTHNOTT, HELLEN, born 1760, wife of Hugh James Patterson Rollo of Bannockburn, Stirlingshire, died in 1838. [St John's gravestone, Edinburgh]

ARBUTHNOTT, Sir WILLIAM, born 1767, died 1829, husband of Lady Anne, born 1778, died in 1846. [St John's gravestone, Edinburgh]

ARMOUR, JOHN, son of John Armour, a merchant in Edinburgh, died at Heywood Hall, St Mary's, Jamaica, on 30 April 1805. [SM.67.566]

ARMSTRONG, THOMAS, younger son of William Armstrong in Niddry Street, Edinburgh, died in St Ann's, Jamaica, in April 1821. [SM][DPCA][BM.10.609]

ARNOT, WILLIAM, a blacksmith, [1795-1836], husband of Margaret Campbell, [179- - 1869]. [South Leith gravestone]

ARTHUR, WILLIAM, born 1799, a cooper, with his wife Margaret and a child, emigrated from Leith on the Symmetry, master William Cochrane, bound for Buenos Ayres, Argentina, on 22 May 1825, landed there on 11 August 1825. [SRP.18]

ASHENHEIM, JACOB, a jeweller 103 Princes Street, Edinburgh, in 1849. [POD]

ATHILL, MARY, daughter of James Athill in Antigua, married Lewis Evans, a surgeon in London, in Edinburgh on 22 July 1823. [S.370.480]

ATKINSON, Miss E., milliner and dress maker, 27 Hanover Street, Edinburgh, 1849. [POD]

ATKINSON, Sir GEORGE, MD, born in 1762, died in 1832. [St John's gravestone, Edinburgh]

ATTWELL, WILLIAM, born 1782, a basket maker, with his wife Agnes and five children, emigrated from Leith on the Symmetry, master William Cochrane, bound for Buenos Ayres, Argentina, on 22 May 1825, landed there on 11 August 1825. [SRP.18]

AUCHINCLOSS, J., smith, 19 Rose Street, Edinburgh, 1849. [POD]

AUCHTERLONIE, JOHN, second son of John Auchterlonie of Infirmary Street, Edinburgh, died in Kingston, Jamaica, on 1 February 1827. [BM.22.265]

AULD, WILLIAM, born 1770, a surgeon in Edinburgh, who emigrated to Hudson Bay, in 1790, aboard the Seahorse, a Hudson Bay Company employee at Churchill Factory from 1790 until 1815, eldest son of Robert Auld of the Edinburgh Foundry, appointed John Elder, a writer in Edinburgh, and Robert Auld, his brother in Edinburgh, as his factors and attornies in 1802, died in Edinburgh after 1830. [NRS.RD4.272.723] [HBRS]

AULD, WILLIAM, a boot and shoemaker, 513 Lawnmarket, Edinburgh, 1849. [POD]

AUSTIN, JAMES, MD, from Barbados, married Elizabeth Mary Pierce, only daughter of William Pierce in Jamaica, in Edinburgh on 4 September 1820. [BM.8.119]

AYTOUN, PATRICK, a merchant in Kingston, Jamaica, second son of William Aytoun a Writer to the Signet, appointed his brother Roger Aytoun, a Writer to the Signet in Edinburgh, as his attorney, in 1789. [NRS.RD4.250.160]

BAIGRIE, Miss, eldest daughter of Mackenzie Baigrie in Edinburgh, married Alexander McLean from Orangehill, Jamaica, in London on 30 April 1819. [S.119.19]

BAILLIE, GEORGE, born 1786, a surgeon on the Bengal Establishment, died on 3 July 1854, husband of Flora Loudon, born 1800, died 7 May 1833. [St Cuthbert's gravestone]

BAILLIE, JOHN, a surgeon in Edinburgh, later in Demerara, a deed on 13 April 1824, [NRS.RD4.383-394]; died on 12 August 1829, testament, 1830, Edinburgh. [NRS]

BAILLIE, SUTTIE, from Edinburgh, died in Demerara in 1801. [AJ.2825]

BAILLIE, WILLIAM, a tailor in Edinburgh, versus his wife Ann White, a Process of Divorce in 1807. [NRS.CC8.5.29]

BAIRD, RICHARD FREDERICK, youngest son of Sir James Gardiner Baird of Saughtonhall, died in Bermuda on 15 June 1819. [EA] [AJ.3731][S.131.19]

BAKKE, JANET, wife of James Adams a tinsmith from Leith, died in Huntingdon, Leith, in 1854. [S.23.4.1854]

BALFOUR, HELEN, eldest daughter of Charles Balfour in Jamaica, married John Tennant from Virginia, in Edinburgh in May 1794. [EA.3167.286]

BALGARNIE, WILLIAM, born 1846, from Edinburgh, died in George town, Demerara, on 31 July 1873. [S.9388]; father of a daughter born in Valparaiso, Chile, on 27 August 1871. [S.8804]

BALLANTYNE, JAMES BURN, born 1829, son of William Ballantyne, a teacher in Edinburgh, the assessor of Kinnley County, died in Brackett, Texas, on 4 December 1877. [St Cuthbert's gravestone]

BALLENDEN, JOHN, born 1755, an employee of the Hudson Bay Company, who died in Stromness, Orkney, on 23 May 1817. [New Calton gravestone]

BALLINGALL, Mrs, an artificial flower and feather maker in Northwest Circus Place, Edinburgh, in 1849. [POD]

BALMAINE, ALEXANDER, born 1740 in Edinburgh, was educated at the Universities of St Andrews and of Edinburgh from 1757 until 1760, emigrated to America in 1772, was an assistant minister at Copley, Virginia, in 1772, later in the parishes of Augusta and Frederick, Virginia, husband of Lucy Taylor, died in 1820. [EMA.12] [FPA.310/330] [OC.319] [VJ.23.11.1788]

BALMAIN, ANDREW, a merchant, son of John Balmain a writer in Edinburgh, died in New York on 14 September 1799. [GC.1323]

BALMAIN, Misses, milliners and dress makers, 21 Charlotte Street, Leith, 1849. [POD]

BALCANQUELL, ROBERT GEORGE, from Edinburgh, then a planter in St John's parish, Middlesex County, Jamaica, appointed Thomas Hewen, formerly a Captain of H M Dragoons, in Edinburgh, as his attorney in 1793. [NRS.RD4.254.934]

BANKS, BESSIE, born 1847, third daughter of John Banks of 50 South Bridge, Edinburgh, died in Belize on 29 August 1869. [S.8164]

BANKS, WALTER, born 1838 in Edinburgh, died in Rosario de Santa Fe, Argentina, on 25 January 1869. [S.8002]

BANKS, WILLIAM, in Edinburgh, a deed, 24 December 1841. [NRS.RD29.3.23]

BANNERMAN, Miss, an embroiderer, 4 North St James Street, Edinburgh, 1849. [POD]

BARBER, MARGARET, born 1800, a servant, emigrated from Leith on the Symmetry, master William Cochrane, bound for Buenos Ayres, Argentina, on 22 May 1825, landed there on 11 August 1825. [SRP.18]

BARCLAY, ROBERT, born 1802, a servant, with his wife Helen and a child, emigrated from Leith on the Symmetry, master William Cochrane, bound for Buenos Ayres, Argentina, on 22 May 1825, landed there on 11 August 1825. [SRP.18]

BARCLAY, ROBINA, wife of Walter Turnbull in Hanover, Jamaica, died on 24 September 1842. [Greyfriars gravestone, Edinburgh]

BARKER, JONATHAN, born 1785, a bricklayer, with his wife Elizabeth and two children, emigrated from Leith on the Symmetry, master William Cochrane, bound for Buenos Ayres, Argentina, on 22 May 1825, landed there on 11 August 1825. [SRP.18]

BARKER, PETER, a shipmaster in Leith, testament, 1804, Comm. Edinburgh. [NRS.CC8.8.135.305]

BARKER, THOMAS, elder of South Leith parish in 1825. [SLR]; a brewer in Leith, a petitioner in 1828; an elder on 1 October 1843. [SLR]

BARLAS, R., a land valuator, 18 Gilmore Place, Edinburgh, in 1849. [POD]

BARNETSON, Miss, toy warehouse, 76 Princes Street, Edinburgh, 1849. [POD]

BARNSTON, ROBERT, born 1800 in Edinburgh, emigrated to Canada, an employee of the North West Company from 1820 to 1820, later an employee of the Hudson Bay Company from 1821 to 1863. [HBRS]

BARR, CHARLES, a shipmaster in Leith, inventory and testament, 1814. [NRS]

BARTLEMAN, JOHN, a Major of the Royal Marines, born 1771, died on 2 January 1827. [Grayfriars gravestone]

BEATSON, ROBERT, spirit dealer, 41 Shore, Leith, 1849. [POD]

BEATSON, W. D., late in Edinburgh, died in Georgetown, Demerara, on 29 July 1867. [FH]

BEATTIE, MAXWELL, born 1804, a servant, emigrated from Leith on the Symmetry, master William Cochrane, bound for Buenos Ayres, Argentina, on 22 May 1825, landed there on 11 August 1825. [SRP.18]

BEAVIS, JOHN, a plumber from Edinburgh, died in Mexico on 20 June 1867. [S.7512]

BECK, KERR, and Company, wholesale merchants and tenants in the Bush, Leith, in 1811. [LD]

BEGBIE, ALEXANDER, a plumber and glazier in Leith, journals from 1797 to 1804. [NRS.CS96.14]

BEGBIE, WILLIAM, a lapidary, 8 St James's Square, Edinburgh, in 1849. [POD]

BEGLIE, ALEXANDER, a surgeon in Surinam, a sasine, 1831. [NRS.R.S.Edinburgh 38.174]

BELCH, PETER, an advocate from Edinburgh, died in Kingston, Jamaica, on 8 March 1808. [SM.70.477]

BELL, JAMES, eldest son of George Bell in North Leith, married Dorcas Langton, second daughter of James Langton of Bruree, County Limerick, Ireland, in San Francisco, California, on 3 June 1854. [W.XV.1568]

BELL, JOHN, a grocer in Nicolson Street, Edinburgh, died on 22 August 1822. [SM.90.520]

BELL, JOHN EDWARD, second son of James Bell, a Solicitor to the Supreme Court, North Bridge, Edinburgh, was killed at Tucuman, Argentina, on 1 December 1876. [S.0420]

BELL, WILLIAM, formerly a merchant in Charleston, South Carolina, later in Edinburgh, married Isabella Dempster, in Edinburgh on 27 July 1815. [EMR]

BELL, WILLIAM, mill-master, Canonmills, Edinburgh, 1849. [POD]

BENNETT, ANDREW, of Muckraw, farmer at Brunston, died 10 February 1824, husband of Marion Horn, died 1793, parents of John Bennett who died in Malta. [Duddingston gravestone]

BENNETT, ARCHIBALD, of Muckraw, born 1783, Secretary of the Bank of Scotland, died 19 January 1868. [Duddingston gravestone]

BENTLEY, ANTONIA, born 1782, widow of Dr Paul Weston of Charleston, South Carolina, died in Portobello in 1857. [Greyfriars gravestone, Edinburgh]

BENTLEY, PENELOPE, daughter of Bentley Gordon Bentley, and wife of Dr Hazell in South Carolina, died in Edinburgh on 23 July 1809. [SM.71.640]

BERRY, FANNY, daughter of Dr Andrew Berry in Edinburgh, married Josiah Webb Archibald, from Puerto Rico, in the Protestant Church of La Tour, Piedmont, France, on 20 October 1825. [BM.18.779]

BERRY, JAMES, a saddle and harness maker, 13 Bread Street, Edinburgh, 1849. [POD]

BERRY, MOSES, born 1803, a carpenter, who emigrated from Leith aboard the Symmetry bound for Buenos Ayres, Argentina, on 22 May 1825, landed there on 11 August 1825. [SRP.19]

BERTIE, JAMES, eldest son of James Bertie of Brechin and Edinburgh, married Victorina Carrera, only daughter of James Carrera of Gibraltar, in Rosario de Santa Fe, Argentina, on 24 October 1879. [S.11371]

BERTRAM, MARY, widow of John Smith in St Elizabeth, Jamaica, died in 76 Nicolson Street, Edinburgh, on 29 October 1825. [S.609.719]

BERWICK, A., brewer, 122 Canongate, Edinburgh, 1849. [POD]

BERWICK, JOHN BONNAR, born 1829, sixth son of William Bonnar in Edinburgh, died in Toronto, Ontario, on 22 April 1873. [EC.27647]

BEUGO, JOHN, born 7 May 1759, an engraver, died on 13 December 1841, husband of Elizabeth McDowall, born 25 March 1764, died on 16 June 1849. [Greyfriars gravestone]

BEVERIDGE, JOHN, in Edinburgh, a deed, 12 April 1841. [NRS.RD29.3.23]

BINNIE, JOHN, born 1793 in Edinburgh, died 6 December 1830. [Kingston Cathedral gravestone, Jamaica]

BISHOP, GEORGE, master of the Skeen of Leith from Leith to Halifax, Nova Scotia, and Quebec in 1819. [NRS.E504.22.84]

BISHOP, J., master of the Traveller of Leith from Leith bound for Halifax, Nova Scotia, in 1817. [NRS.E504.22.77]

BISSET, JAMES SOMERVAIL, son of Adam Bisset in Leith, died at Spring Garden, Jamaica, on 12 June 1826. [BM.20.655]

BISSETT, ROBERT, in Leith, applied to settle in Canada on 1 March 1815. [NRS.RH9]

BLACK, FRANCIS, born 1782, son of Charles Black, [1756-1826], a builder, and his wife Isabella Nicol, [1750-1849], died in Kingston, Jamaica, in October 1812. [Greyfriars gravestone, Edinburgh]

BLACK, GEORGE, a sailmaker in Sydney, Australia, son and heir of James Black, a ropemaker in Leith, and his wife Margaret Scott in 1856. [NRS.S/H]

BLACK, Captain J., master of the Ossian of Leith, from Greenock to New York in 1821; from Greenock via Fort William to Quebec in 1822. [NRS.E504.15.138] [QM.28.8.1822]

BLACK, JAMES, a tobacconist in Leith, was admitted as a burgess and guilds-brother of Dunfermline on 13 August 1793. [DM]

BLACK, JOHN, probably from Edinburgh, settled in Laurens District of South Carolina by 1809. [NRS.CS17.1.28/498]

BLACK, ROBERT, of Easter Portsburgh, died 16 March 1790, his wife Rachel Ray, died 8 March 1798, parents of James Black in Philadelphia, Pennsylvania. [St Cuthbert's gravestone, Edinburgh]

BLACK, WILLIAM, probably from Edinburgh, settled in Laurens District of South Carolina by 1809. [NRS.CS17.1.28/498]

BLACKIE, WALTER, in Edinburgh, a contract of marriage with Mrs H. Brodie, 24 Aril 1841. [NRS.RD29.3.23]

BLADWORTH, R., an iron-founder, 67 North Bridge, Edinburgh, in 1849. [POD]

BLADWORTH, WILLIAM, born 1775, a merchant in Edinburgh, died on 18 March 1847, husband of Jean Preston, born 1777, died on 28 February 1860. [St Cuthbert's gravestone, Edinburgh]

BOAK, WILLIAM, tanner, 57 Westport, Edinburgh, 1849. [POD]

BOGIE, Miss, a lace cleaner, 22 Rose Street, Edinburgh, in 1849. [POD]

BOGLE, THOMAS, eldest son of Jacob Bogle, a police lieutenant in Edinburgh, died in Trinidad in March 1818. [BM.3.630]

BONAR, DAVID, tailor, 2 Crichton Street, Edinburgh, 1849. [POD]

BONE, HELEN, born 1800, a servant who emigrated from Leith aboard the Symmetry bound for Buenos Ayres, Argentina, on 22 May 1825, landed there on 11 August 1825. [SRP.19]

BONE, MAGDALENE, from Edinburgh, died in Port Dalhousie, Upper Canada, in 1854. [S.9.9.1854]

BONNALIE, SAMUEL J., born 18 August 1826, died 8 December 1858. [St Cuthbert's gravestone, Edinburgh]

BONNAR, THOMAS, of 77 George Street, Edinburgh, father of Kate Bonnar who married William Ogilvie, an accountant, on Staten Island, New York, on 4 October 1868. [S.7870]

BONTHRON, JOHN, born 1777, son of James Bonthron a builder in Edinburgh, a merchant in Charleston, South Carolina, died there on 20 June 1817. [Old Scots gravestone, Charleston] [BM.1.671]

BORROWMAN, ALEXANDER, born 1820, fifth son of Robert Borrowman and Elizabeth Stevenson, died in Montreal, Quebec, on 17 December 1884. [Greyfriars gravestone]

BORROWMAN, ROBERT, born 1784, died on 8 December 1837, husband of Elizabeth Stevenson, born 1789, died on 4 May 1841. [Greyfriars gravestone]

BORROWMAN, THOMSON, born 1824, sixth son of Robert Borrowman and Elizabeth Stevenson, died in Valparaiso, Chile, on 26 August 1876. [Greyfriars gravestone]

BORSTELL, W., German teacher, 6 Mansfield Place, Edinburgh, 1849. [POD]

BORTHWICK, GEORGE, a smith, late from Jamaica, now in Fountainbridge, Edinburgh, 1799. [NRS.CS22.776.8]

BORTHWICK and GOUDIE, weavers in Belhaven, East Lothian, a partner absconded to America, sederunt books, 1822-1836. [NRS.CS96.326-332]

BOSWELL, JOHN SANDEMAN, born 1810, a Captain of the Bengal Army, died in India on 29 October 1840. [Greyfriars gravestone]

BOSWELL, WILLIAM HENRY, born 1816, a Major of the Madras Army, died in India on 7 June 1857. [Greyfriars gravestone]

BOYD, ALEXANDER, son of William Boyd in South Leith, settled in Savannah, Georgia, probate, December 1804, PCC. [TNA]

BOYD, JAMES, a merchant in Edinburgh, sederunt book from 1814 to 1817 mentions army deserters in America. [NRS.CS96.830]

BOYD, ROBERT, born 1804, a servant who emigrated from Leith aboard the Symmetry bound for Buenos Ayres, Argentina, on 22 May 1825, landed there on 11 August 1825. [SRP.19]

BOYES, ROBERT, of 22 Gardner's Crescent, Edinburgh, Captain in the Service of the East India Company, died 10 November 1834, an inventory, 1835. [NRS]

BOYLE, CATHERINE, wife of William Paterson a plumber, from Edinburgh, died in Mexico on 24 December 1876. [S.10,464]

BOYNE, JAMES, a hatter, 16 Sandport Street, Leith, 1849. [POD]

BRADFOOT, MARY, born 1769, widow of Captain John Graham, died on 6 December 1832. [Greyfriars gravestone]

BRANDER, G., a tin plate worker, 5 Carruber's Close, Edinburgh, 1849. [POD]

BRANDER, WILLIAM, in Trelawney, Jamaica, appointed his brother Martin Brander, a gunsmith in London, and George Andrews, a writer in Edinburgh, as his attornies, in 1794, deed refers to his grand-uncle Martin Brander, formerly in London later in Fisherow, Edinburgh, father of William Brander. [NRS.RD4.255.660]

BREBNER, JOHN, from Leith, a merchant in Halifax, Nova Scotia, in 1786. [NRS.CS17.1.5.224]

BRECK, JOHN, a house painter, 34 Castle Street, Edinburgh, 1849. [POD]

BREMNER, GEORGE, a shoemaker in Edinburgh, and his wife Janet Brown, a Process of Divorce in 1826. [NRS.CC8.6.152]

BREMNER, JOSEPH, a mariner in Leith, testament, 1793, Comm. Edinburgh. [NRS]

BRIDGES, JAMES, sixth son of Francis Bridges in Edinburgh, died in Berbice on 9 September 1846. [EEC.21413]

BRIDGES, PETER, son of Francis Bridges in Edinburgh, formerly in Demerara, died in New South Wales, Australia, on 18 December 1877. [EC.29134]

BRIGGS, THOMAS, a skipper in Leith, testament, 8 February 1797, Comm. Edinburgh. [NRS]

BRISCO, MARY, only daughter of Thomas Brisco in Jamaica, married Lieutenant E. Payne of the 75th Regiment, in Edinburgh, on 10 September 1819. [DPCA.894]

BROACH, JAMES, born 1801, a farmer, with his sister, emigrated via Leith on the Symmetry bound for Buenos Ayres, Argentina, on 22 May 1825, landed there on 11 August 1825. [SRP.18]

BROADFOOT, WALLACE, second son of John Bradfoot a merchant in Leith, and stepson of Reverend R. W. Thomson in Kim, died on Zeelght Plantation, Demerara, on 5 January 1871. [S.8583]; a planter in Demerara, testament, 1871, Edinburgh. [NRS.SC70.1.154/707]

BROCKIE, JAMES, a sailor, testament, 1801, Comm. Edinburgh. [NRS]

BRODIE, ALEXANDER, a corn merchant and tenant in the Bush, Leith, in 1811. [LD]

BRODIE, ALEXANDER OSWALD, born 1788, a merchant in New York, died in Edinburgh on 9 September 1856. [GM.ns2/1.526]

BRODIE, ELIZABETH, spouse of John Ferguson a tide-waiter in Leith, versus Archibald Stewart, junior, a merchant in Edinburgh, 17…….. [NRS.CS228.B.4.11]

BRODIE, JANET WALKER, born 1789, died in 1874. [St John's gravestone, Edinburgh]

BRODIE, W., a sculptor, 10 St Andrew Street, Edinburgh, 1849. [POD]

BRODIE, WILLIAM, [1815-1881], and his wife Helen Chisholm, [1817-1886], parents of James Buchanan Brodie who died in Corvallis, Oregon, on 22 November 1915. [Dean gravestone, Edinburgh]

BROLOCHAN, A., victual dealer and provision merchant, 319 High Street, Edinburgh, 1849. [POD]

BROTCHIE, ROBERT, merchant, 8 Mitchell Street, Edinburgh, 1849. [POD]

BROWN, ADAM, born 1781 in Edinburgh, a mariner who was naturalised in Charleston, South Carolina, on 11 October 1804. [NARA.M1183.1]

BROWN, ANDREW, formerly a merchant in Leith, died in New York on 1 August 1828. [BM.25.268]

BROWN, DAVID, in Forsyth's Land, South Leith, was granted a beggar's badge on 18 February 1794. [SLR]

BROWN, DAVID, a ship's carpenter in Leith, testament, 1805, Comm. Edinburgh. [NRS]

BROUN, ELIZABETH, in Tods Hole, South Leith, was granted a beggar's badge on 18 February 1794. [SLR]

BROWN, JAMES, born 1800, a servant, with Mary, his wife, and child, emigrated from Leith to Buenos Ayres, Argentina, on the Symmetry, on 22 May 1825, landed there on 11 August 1825. [SRP.19]

BROWN, JAMES, born 1799, a servant who emigrated from Leith aboard the Symmetry bound for Buenos Ayres, Argentina, on 22 May 1825, landed there on 11 August 1825. [SRP.19]

BROWN, JAMES, a gardener from Edinburgh, emigrated to Poyais, died in Belize in 1823. [EEC.17520]

BROWN, JANET, born 1799, a servant who emigrated from Leith aboard the Symmetry bound for Buenos Ayres, Argentina, on 22 May 1825, landed there on 11 August 1825. [SRP.19]

BROWN, JOHN, a shipmaster in Leith, accounts of the Lovely Mary of Leith from 1791 to 1792, [NRS.CS96.4493]; trading with Christiansund in 1790s, [NRS.CS.239.T14.45]; testament, 1825, Comm. Edinburgh. [NRS]

BROWN, PATRICK, born 1750, son of Malcolm Brown a merchant, formerly Captain of the 25th Regiment of Foot, died on 8 August 1808, husband of Elizabeth Home, born 1758, died on 25 April 1842. [Greyfriars gravestone]

BROWN, ROBERT, a merchant and tenant in the Bush, Leith, in 1811. [LD]

BROWN, ROBERT, a shipmaster in Leith, testament, 1822, Comm. Edinburgh. [NRS]

BROWN, WALTER, in Exuma, the Bahamas, a deed re his wife Elizabeth Walker, his brother James Brown a staymaster in Edinburgh, his brother-in-law Francis Marshall a merchant in Edinburgh, Martin Jollie in Edinburgh, subscribed in Edinburgh on 1 September 1801, witnessed by William Wilson and James Gibson, clerks. [NRS.RD5.48.399]

BROWN, WALTER, in 20 Bernard Street, Leith, a letter to the South Leith Kirk Session re the burial ground of the Incorporation of Wrights and Mason of South Leith, 12 January 1835. [SLR]

BRUCE, ANDREW, in Alleghany County, Maryland, son of the late Charles Bruce in Edinburgh, appointed his cousin James Green in Muirkirk, as his attorney in 1795, refers to William Brechin, a Writer to the Signet in Edinburgh. [NRS.RD3.276.1090]

BRUCE, DAVID, born in Edinburgh, emigrated to America in 1793, a publisher in New York, died in Brooklyn, N.Y. in 1857. [ANY]

BRUCE, JAMES, an organ builder, 6 North Bank Street, Edinburgh, 1849. [POD]

BRUCE, JAMES, a coach-bodymaker in Edinburgh, father of James Constable Bruce, born 1865, died in Brooklyn, New York, on 24 October1884. [S.12899]

BRUCE, MARY, daughter of James Bruce of the Naval Office in Leith, married William Henry Street, of St John's, New Brunswick, on 15 March 1824. [FH.107]

BRUCE, Mrs, widow of James Bruce the Naval Officer in Leith, died in St John, New Brunswick, on 4 February 1834. [NBC.8.2.1834]

BRYCE, NICHOL, baptised on 11 November 1780 in St Cuthbert's, Edinburgh, son of William Bryce and his wife Janet Scott, a merchant who was naturalised in Charleston, South Carolina, on 16 September 1805. [NARA.M1183.1]

BRYDEN, JOSEPH, born 1815, late of 6 Pitt Street, Edinburgh, died at the Cape of Good Hope, South Africa, on 23 February 1840. [EEC.20047]

BRYDEN, WILLIAM, born 1789, a writer in Edinburgh, died 14 December 1819. [SM.85]

BRYDON, G., a haberdasher, 261 High Street, Edinburgh, 1849. [POD]

BRYSON, PETER, from Leith, married Mary Smith, second daughter of James Smith in Kinleith, Currie, Midlothian, in Valparaiso, Chile, on 28 September 1869. [S.8206]; parents of a daughter born there on 3 October 1871. [S.8842]; also, of a son born there on 16 February 1873. [S.9308]

BUCHAN, DAVID HUME, died at the head of Bruntsfield Links, Edinburgh, on 19 September 1822. [SM.90.632]

BUCHANAN, ARTHUR, born 1820, son of Colin Buchanan in Barbados, educated at Edinburgh Academy from 1828 to 1829. [EAR]

BUCHANAN, COLIN, born 1818, son of Colin Buchanan in Barbados, was educated at Edinburgh Academy from 1828 to 1829. [EAR]

BUCHANAN, DUNCAN, born 1739, formerly a surgeon in Madras, India, died on 18 February 1809. [Grayfriars gravestone]

BUCHANAN, DUNCAN, born 1805, second son of John Buchanan, in the Service of the East India Company, died on 20 October 1855, husband of Janetta Fraser Robertson. [Grayfriars gravestone]

BUCHANAN, HENRY, from Edinburgh, in Toronto, Ontario, or in the State of New York, a sasine, 30 January 1848. [NRS.RS.Edinburgh.46.125]

BUCHANAN, JOHN, first son of Duncan Buchanan late of Madras, India, died on 24 October 1836. [Grayfriars gravestone]

BUCKHAM, ANDREW, born 1780 in Edinburgh, a physician in New York, died there on 21 April 1844. [ANY]

BUIE, ALEXANDER, born 1815, died on Florence Estate, Jamaica, on 10 February 1857. [New Calton gravestone, Edinburgh]

BULLOCK, J., spirit dealer, 20 High Street, Edinburgh, 1849. [POD]

BUNCLE, ALEXANDER, born 1802, a cooper who emigrated via Leith on the brig Magnet to Charleston, South Carolina, in 1828. [NARA]

BURGES, ABIAL, master of the Hannibal of Newburg Port, Massachusetts appointed David Jamieson, William Gibson, and Robert Gibson, merchants in Leith as his attorneys, deed written by Alexander Orchison, clerk to William Smith a Solicitor of the Supreme Court of Scotland, was subscribed in Edinburgh on 11 July 1812, and witnessed by William Smith and Alexander Orchiston. [NRS.RD5.37.262]

BURLIN, Dr FRANCIS, from Edinburgh, in the Service of the East India Company, died on 23 August 1841, an inventory, 1843. [NRS]

BURNS, GEORGE, Doctor of Divinity, minister of the Scots Church in St John, New Brunswick, married Esther Struthers, daughter of Reverend James Struthers of the College Chapel in Edinburgh, in St Andrews on 6 August 1827. [BM.22.527]; their daughter was born in St John on 10 August 1828. [BM.24.804]

BURN, HANNAH, daughter of James Burn of the Mint, Edinburgh, and wife of ..... Mackintosh, a general merchant in Fredericton, New Brunswick, died in St John, N.B., on 7 June 1828. [BM.24.407]

BURNS, MICHAEL, born 6 January 1818, a coalmaster, died 3 May 1888. [St Cuthbert's gravestone, Edinburgh]

BURNS, WALTER, born 1778, an upholsterer, died on 14 March 1838, husband of Christian Bruce, born 1778, died on 27 May 1813. [Greyfriars gravestone]

BURNET, ALEXANDER, elder of South Leith parish in 1825. [SLR]; a merchant in Leith, a petitioner in 1828. [SLR]

BURTON, ROBERT, in Richmond, Virginia, appointed John Burton his brother in Leith, as his attorney on 23 April 1805. [NRS.RD3.309/1.682]

BUSHER, JOHN, a gold beater, 56 Thistle Street, Edinburgh, 1849. [POD]

BUTCHART, JOHN, a timber merchant in Quebec, appointed Henry Johnston Wyllie in Edinburgh as his attorney in 1819, deed subscribed in Edinburgh on 16 January 1819, written by John McCraken a clerk, and witnessed by George Crossbie, a merchant in Edinburgh, and said John McCraken. [NRS.RD5.10]; he discharged his attorney on 9 March 1821. [NRS.RD5.198.295]

BUTLER, WILLIAM, a shoemaker in Edinburgh, possibly emigrated to America in 1812. [NRS.CS233, Seqn.B1,34]

BUTTERS, L., a seal engraver, 41 George Street, Edinburgh, 1849. [POD]

BYCROFT, T., a comb maker in Bull's Close, Canongate, Edinburgh, 1849. [POD]

CADELL, WILLIAM, in Edinburgh, a letter re James Stuart of Dunearn a Writer to the Signet, a debtor who had absconded to America, in 1828. [NRS.GD180.685.1]

CALDER, ALEXANDER, born 1773 in Edinburgh, was naturalised in Charleston, South Carolina, on 25 March 1803. [NARA.M1183.1]

CALDER, WILLIAM, youngest son of Alexander Calder in Edinburgh, married Mary Elizabeth Williams, daughter of ..... Williams in Berbice, there on 15 April 1869. [S.8063]

CALLENDAR, JAMES, born on 4 June 1829 in Leith, emigrated to New York in 1850, a merchant there , died in Brooklyn on 23 April 1903] [ANY]

CALLUM, JOHN REID, born 1844, eldest son o John Callum, a merchant in Edinburgh, died in Georgetown, Demerara, on 29 October 1862. [S.2329]

CALVERT, F., a porter storehouseman and tenant in the Bush, Leith, in 1811. [LD]

CAMERON, ANDREW, a drysalter, 47 Regent Arch, Edinburgh, 1849. [POD]

CAMERON, ARCHIBALD, born 1778, a boot and shoe merchant, died on 14 March 1846, husband of Jane Henderson, born 1790, died on 1 December 1868. [Greyfriars gravestone]

CAMERON, ROBERT, from Edinburgh, in America by 1796. [NRS.CS17.1.15/267]

CAMPBELL, ALEXANDER, an author in 6 Lothian Street, Edinburgh, a letter in 1838. [NRS.GD113.5.499.52]

CAMPBELL, CHRISTINA, youngest daughter of D. Campbell in Leith, married Simon Kerr of the English Academy in Coquimba, Chile, on 30 March 1861. [S.1842]; later in Serana, Chile, testament, Edinburgh, 1876. [NRS.SC70.1.177/10]

CAMPBELL, DANIEL, second son of John Campbell, a merchant in Edinburgh, died at St Ann's Bay, Jamaica, on 22 May 1793. [SM.55.360]

CAMPBELL, DUNCAN, a mariner in the Royal Navy, testament, 1791, Comm. Edinburgh. [NRS]

CAMPBELL, General DUNCAN, born 29 June 1763, Colonel of the 91st [Argyll] Regiment, died on 9 April 1837. [Greyfriars gravestone]

CAMPBELL, Mrs GRACE, widow of Alexander Campbell, late of Tobago, died in Edinburgh on 12 December 1823. [SM]

CAMPBELL, ISABEL, in Lamb's Court, South Leith, was granted a beggar's badge on 18 February 1794. [SLR]

CAMPBELL, JAMES, in York Place, Edinburgh, a Lieutenant Colonel in the Service of the East India Company, died 23 September 1836, inventory 1836. [NRS]

CAMPBELL, JOHN, of the Commissary Department, son of Patrick Campbell of the Royal Bank of Scotland in Edinburgh, died in Berbice on 10 December 1805. [SM.68.78] [EEC.1806] [AJ.3044]

CAMPBELL, JOHN, born in Edinburgh, son of John Campbell of the Citadel and his wife Anne Caroline, died in Geneva, Switzerland, on 11 August 1829. [Canongait gravestone]

CAMPBELL, ROBERT, born in Edinburgh, a bookseller and stationer, died in Philadelphia, Pennsylvania, on 14 August 1800. [SM.62.779]

CAMPBELL, SAMUEL, born 1737 in Edinburgh, died in New York on 17 April 1813. [EA.5172.13] [SM.75.639] [EEC.1813]

CAMPBELL, SAMUEL, born 18 July 1765, son of Samuel Campbell, a bookbinder, and his wife Catherine Taylor, a bookseller in New York, died there on 26 June 1836. [ANY]

CAMPBELL, THOMAS, a sailor in Leith, testament, 10 March 1790, Comm. Edinburgh. [NRS]

CAMPBELL, WILLIAM PATRICK, born 10 January 1819, son of William Campbell a merchant in USA, educated at Edinburgh Academy from 1828 to 1829. [EAR]

CANDLISH, JOHN BOGLE, born 2 November 1837 in Edinburgh, son of Reverend Robert Smith and his wife Jessie Brocks, an insurance agent in Australia. [F.1.106]

CARFRAE, M., a bird and animal stuffer of 13 Frederick Street, Edinburgh, in 1849. [POD]

CARGILL, WILLIAM, born 1784 in Edinburgh, son of James Cargill and his wife Marion Jamieson, a British soldier from 1802 to 1820, Captain of the 7th Regiment, married Mary Ann Yates, emigrated to New Zealand in 1847, founded Otago, a politician, died in Dunedin on 6 August 1860. [Otago Settlers Museum, N.Z.]

CARMICHAEL, MARY, in Edinburgh, sister of Henry Carmichael in New South Wales, Australia, in 1857. [NRS.S/H]

CARSON, SAMUEL, MD, from St John, Newfoundland, married Margaret Sawers, youngest daughter of Reverend William Sawers, MA, minister of Crookham, Northumberland, in Edinburgh on 7 January 1830. [BM.28.571]

CARSTAIRS, GEORGE STEWART, of Potosi, born 1810, formerly a merchant in Leith, died on Plantation Caledonia in Surinam on 7 June 1842. [EEC.20408]

CARSTAIRS, JAMES, a nurseryman, seedsman and florist, Warriston Lodge, Edinburgh, 1849. [POD]

CASSELS, ANDREW, in Leith, father of Andrew Cassels the King's Advocate at the Cape of Good Hope, died in Cape Town, South Africa, on 7 January 1809. [SM.71.318]

CASSELS, HANNAH, daughter of Andrew Cassels, a merchant in Leith, married David Brown, a merchant in St Petersburg, Russia, on 21 June 1791, in Leith, [SM.53.307]; born 1762, she died on 7 March 1859. [Greyfriars gravestone, Edinburgh]

CASTLE, JAMES, a working jeweller, 21 Leith Street, Edinburgh, in 1849. [POD]

CATHCART, JAMES, born 1802, a surveyor who emigrated from Leith to Buenos Ayres, Argentina, on the Symmetry on 22 May 1825, landed there on 11 August 1825. [SRP.19]

CATTENACH, PETER LORIMER, born 4 November 1832, an advocate, died on 19 May 1905, husband of Jane Bladsworth, born 11 November 1843, and died on 18 January 1895. [St Cuthbert's gravestone]

CAW, ALEXANDER, formerly a merchant in Leith, died in Charleston, South Carolina, on 18 August 1817. [S.42.1817]

CAW, J. B., a goldsmith, 15 North Bridge, Edinburgh, 1849. [POD]

CAY, THOMAS, son of Thomas Cay an advocate in Edinburgh, died at Rosario de Santa Fe, Argentina, on 25 February 1868. [S.7690]; testament, 1871, Edinburgh. [NRS.SC70.1.153/39]

CHALMERS, GLASSFORD, youngest son of William Chalmers of Dalry a surgeon in Edinburgh, died in Whitehall, Jamaica, on 6 September 1817. [BM.4.117]

CHALMERS, J., vinegar maker, 39 Potterrow, Edinburgh, 1849. [POD]

CHALMERS, JAMES, in Savanna, Georgia, brother and heir of Margaret Chalmers in Edinburgh, who died on 25 August 1877. [NRS.S/H]

CHALMERS, L., a picture cleaner and liner, 8 Barony Street, Edinburgh, 1849. [POD]

CHALMERS, WALTER, son of James Chalmers a solicitor in Edinburgh, died on Hampden Estate, Jamaica, on 6 August 1827. [BM.23.663]

CHALMERS, WATSON, born 1843, fourth son of Richard Chalmers of 6 Mackenzie Place, Edinburgh, died in Rio de Janeiro, Brazil, on 14 Apri l1860. [S.1551]

CHALMERS, WILLIAM, a shipmaster in Leith, testament, 1815, Comm. Edinburgh. [NRS]

CHAPMAN, JOHN, in Washington, Illinois, brother ad heir of Charles Chapman in Edinburgh, who died on 17 August 1865. [NRS.S/H]

CHARLES, WILLIAM, born 1776 in Edinburgh, emigrated to America in 1805, a caricaturist who died in Philadelphia, Pennsylvania, on 29 August 1820. [WA]

CHESNEY, D., a saw maker in Lothian Road, Edinburgh, 1849. [POD]

CHEYNE, JOHN, a surgeon in Leith, a letter, 28 March 1793. [SLR]

CHEYNE, WILLIAM CHEYNE, MD, late in Mexico, eldest son of Stuart Cheyne, a merchant in Edinburgh, died in New York on 10 December 1841. [GH.4067]

CHEYNE, Miss, eldest daughter of Charles Cheyne a merchant in Edinburgh, also grand-niece of Dr George Cheyne, died in Lunenburg, Nova Scotia, on 8 January 1821, at the house of Reverend R. Aitken, Rector of St John's, her brother-in-law. [DPCA][S.5.226][BM.9.363]

CHISHOLM, GEORGE, born 1754 in Leith, died in Calcutta, India, on 20 February 1833. [Scotch Burial Ground gravestone, Calcutta]

CHISHOLM, GEORGE, born 1783 in Edinburgh, a mariner who was naturalised in Charleston, South Carolina, on 20 March 1803. [NARA.M1183.1]

CHRISTIE, DUNCAN, in Montgomery County, New York, nephew and heir of Donald Christie in Edinburgh, in 1836. [NRS.S/H]

CHRISTENMENT or CHRISTIANSEN, CHRISTEN FREDRICH, born 1791 in Copenhagen, Denmark, settled in Leith on 24 June 1811. [EBR.S.115] [ECA.SL115.2.2/67]

CLAPPERTON, JOHN, a grocer and spirit dealer, 263 Cowgate, Edinburgh, 1849. [POD]

CLARK, GEORGE, a butcher in Detroit, Michigan, nephew and heir of William Murray, a smith in Fisher Row, Edinburgh, who died on 30 October 1851. [NRS.S/H]

CLARK, HUGH, son of Alexander Clark of the West Lothian Cavalry and his wife Catherine, was born on 28 March and baptised in St John the Evangelist, Edinburgh, on 29 April 1798. [NRS.CH12.3.26.3]

CLARK, HUGH, at Grand River, Upper Canada, nephew and heir of John Clark, a plasterer in Edinburgh, who died on 13 April 1836. [NRS.S/H]

CLERK, JAMES, MD, married Barbara Stephen, daughter of Reverend John Stephen, LL.D, Rector of Christ Church, New Providence, in the Bahamas, in Edinburgh on 12 September 1820. [EA.5928.183]

CLARKE, JOHN CUTHBERT, MD, a surgeon in the Royal Navy at the British Hospital in Smyrna, Turkey, for 16 years, died on 8 January 1843. [St Cuthbert's gravestone]

CLARK, WILLIAM, of London Street, Edinburgh, married Mrs Drysdale, widow of Andrew Drysdale a merchant in New York, and daughter of James Gibson in Clackmannan, in Edinburgh on 22 November 1827. [EA.6679.759]

CLAYTON, FRANCIS, from Edinburgh, a merchant and planter in Wilmington, New Hanover County, North Carolina, died on 4 October 1790, probate 1790, N.C. [NRS.CC8.8.128.2]

CLAYTON, THOMAS, a plasterer in Edinburgh, brother and heir of Francis Clayton, a merchant in Wilmington, North Carolina, in 1791. [NRS.S/H]

CLEGHORN, ALEXANDER, a shipmaster in Leith, testament, 1804, Comm. Edinburgh. [NRS.CC8.8.135.115]

CLEGHORN, ARCHIBALD, a merchant from Leith, died in New Glasgow, Canada, on 25 September 1840. [EEC.20126]

CLEGHORN, JEAN, in Muckle's Close, South Leith, was granted a beggar's badge on 18 February 1794. [SLR]

CLEGHORN, JAMES, master of the sloop Neptune of Leith in 1825. [NRS.SC12.6.1825.101]

CLEGHORN, WILLIAM, in Montreal, Quebec, brother and heir of Isobel Cleghorn in Edinburgh, in 1841. [NRS.S/H]

CLEGHORN, WILLIAM, in Ellaville, Georgia, brother and heir of Jacky Cleghorn, daughter of Richard Cleghorn in Edinburgh, who died on 17 September 1843; also, heir to his sister, daughter of Richard Cleghorn in Edinburgh, who died on 29 January 1874. [NRS.S/H]

CLEGHORN, WILLIAM, a merchant from Leith, died in New Glasgow, Canada on 26 May 1849. [SG.18.1838] [EEC.21835]

CLERIHUE, JAMES, son of John Clerihue a vintner in Edinburgh, a Captain- Lieutenant of the Bengal Artillery, testament, 1792, Comm. Edinburgh. [NRS]

CLOW, CHRISTINA, born in February 1830 in Edinburgh, died in North Carolina on 22 January 1915. [Cross Creek gravestone, NC]

COBHAM, M., a music teacher, 40 India Street, Edinburgh, 1849. [POD]

COCKBURN, A., a cow feeder, 208 Canongate, Edinburgh, 1849. [POD]

COCKBURN, JAMES, from Edinburgh, a bosun of the Royal Navy, in 1798. [NRS.S/H]

COCKBURN, RICHARD, a wright in Edinburgh, versus his wife Florence Munn, an action for nullity of marriage on grounds of bigamy in 1801. [NRS.CC8.6.72]

COCKBURN, THOMAS, of Rowchester, Berwickshire, born 1723, died in 1787, father of Mary Cockburn, who died on 15 May 1833, and Cecilia Charlotte Cockburn, born 1774, and died on 3May 1834. [St Cuthbert's gravestone, Edinburgh]

COKE, WILLIAM, a bookseller in Leith, versus Robert Wills a bookseller in Charleston, South Carolina, in 1774, [NRS.CS16.1.157]; also, versus Moses McIntyre, a merchant in Leith, 1794. [NRS.CS97.111.160]

COLLIN, LUCAS, son of Thomas Collin in St Croix, Danish West Indies, was indentured for five years to John McKinlay, a merchant in Edinburgh, on 17 October 1799. [ERA]

COLQUHOUN, HELEN AMELIA, youngest daughter of Humphrey Colquhoun in Jamaica, died in Hope Street, Edinburgh, on 15 December 1810. [EA.4904.415]

COLQUHOUN, JOHN, a chain maker in Edinburgh, versus his wife Rachel Gardiner, a Process of Divorce in 1815. [NRS.CC8.6.103]

COLSTON, JAMES, precentor of South Leith in 1843. [SLR]

COMB, ALEXANDER, a slater in Edinburgh, versus his wife Jean Hewart, a Process of Divorce in 1822. [NRS.CC8.6.140]

COMBE, ANDREW, born 1797, a physician from Edinburgh, doctor aboard the Montezuma, an emigrant ship bound from Liverpool to New York in 1847. [NRS.GD297.30-34]

COMBE, JAMES, MD, born 1796, died 14 February 1883. [South Leith Church window]

COMB, JAMES, elder of South Leith parish in 1825. [SLR]; a cooper in Leith, a petitioner in 1828; an elder on 1 October 1843. [SLR]

COMB, WILLIAM, son of Matthew Comb a brewer in Leith, was apprenticed to James Weir, a baker in Edinburgh, for five years on 11 June 1795. [ERA]

CONDIE, J., master of the Rebecca and Sarah of Leith from Leith bound for Pictou, Nova Scotia, in 1805, and from Tobermory bound for Prince Edward Island in 1806. [NRS.E504.35.1][CM.13039]

CONGREVE, or HENDERSON, CHRISTINA, in Jamaica, sister and heir of Balfour Henderson, son of John Henderson, a merchant in Edinburgh, in 1830. [NRS.S/H]

CONGLETON, T., a shipmaster, Old Sugarhouse Close, Leith, 1849. [POD]

CONSTABLE, JAMES, master of the Pharos of Leith, died in Elsinore, Denmark, on 28 November 1816. [SM.79.319]

CONSTABLE, THOMAS, printer, 11 Thistle Street, Edinburgh, 1849. [POD]

COOK, ALEXANDER, a sailor in Leith, husband of Margaret Hay, in 1795. [SL.122]

COOPER, GEORGE, from St Croix in the Danish West Indies, died in Edinburgh, on 16 January 1822. [DPCA.1017]

CORBETT, HENRY, baptised on 11 August 1795 in Canongait, Edinburgh, son of Robert Corbett and his wife Jean Morrison, settled in Columbia, South Carolina, was naturalised in Charleston, S.C., on 18 November 1824. [NARA.M1183.1]

CORMACK, JANETTE, daughter of Alexander Cormack in St John's, Newfoundland, married William Scott from Naples, Italy, in Edinburgh in May 1824. [S.458.344]

COSSAR, ROBERT, son of David Cossar a stabler in Portsburgh, Edinburgh, was apprenticed to Adam Keir, a baker in Edinburgh, for six years, on 31 March 1791. [ERA]

COULSTON, ALEXANDER, was appointed Precentor of South Leith parish in 1829. [SLR]

COUPAR, JAMES, possibly from Leith, by 1794 in America, [NRS.CS17.1.13.44/261]

COUPAR, THOMAS, a boatbuilder in Leith, later a carpenter on HMS Siam, testament, 3 May 1787, Comm. Edinburgh. [NRS]

COWAN, THOMAS, in Edinburgh, father of William Cowan, a brassfounder in St Petersburg, Russia, in 1832. [NRS.S/H]

COWIE, GEORGE, in Edinburgh, a former Sergeant of the 65th Regiment, and an Out-Pensioner of the Royal Hospital in Chelsea, applied to emigrate to Canada in 1818 with his five children. [TNA.CO384.3]

COX, J. a glue manufacturer, 14 Niddry Street, Edinburgh, 1849. [POD]

CRABB, ALEXANDER, a printer in Cincinnati, Ohio, son and heir of John Crabb in the Pleasance, Edinburgh, in 1852. [NRS.S/H]

CRAIG, C. a lock and hinge maker, Rae's Close, Edinburgh, in 1849. [POD]

CRAIG, JAMES, born 1835, late Inspector of the Poor of St Cuthbert's, died in Davos Platz, Switzerland on 17 October 1884. [S.12879]

CRAIGIE, JOHN, in Edinburgh, a Lieutenant Colonel in the Service of the East India Company, died on 23 November 1840, an inventory, 1841. [NRS]

CRAIGIE, MARGARET, youngest daughter of John Craigie in Quebec, died in Edinburgh on 28 June 1823. [EA.6220.151]

CRAWFORD, DAVID, a machine maker, 72 Clerk Sreet, Edinburgh, in 1849. [POD]

CRAWFORD, JAMES, born on 28 January 1796 in Edinburgh, died on 5 December 1873. [St George's gravestone, Port Elizabeth, South Africa]

CRAWFORD, JOHN, a merchant in Leith, was appointed factor to James Neilson in Baltimore, Maryland, on 20 July 1815. [NRS.RD5.84.625]

CRICHTON, A., a print seller, 54 Princes Street, Edinburgh, 1849. [POD]

CRICHTON, ELIZABETH DUNDAS, born 1798, daughter of Patrick Crichton in Gayfield Square, Edinburgh, married William Lambie from Jamaica, in Edinburgh in 1820, [BM.8.3511] died in Kingston, Jamaica, on 20 December 1821. [Kingston Cathedral, Jamaica, gravestone] [St Andrew's gravestone, Jamaica] [BM.11.382]

CRICHTON, MARGARET, in 21 Queen Street, Edinburgh, relict of Alexander Walker of the East India Company, died on 4 October 1836, an inventory, 1836. [NRS]

CROALL, JOHN, a coach and harness maker, Edinburgh, 1849. [POD]

CROMBIE, FRANCIS, from Edinburgh, died in Demerara on 24 April 1807. [SM.69.638]

CROPPER, W., a house painter, 7 India Place, Edinburgh, 1849. [POD]

CROUCH, WILLIAM, a clock and watchmaker, 40 North Bridge Street, Edinburgh, 1849. [POD] [Leith gravestone]

CROWDEN, PETER, a skipper in Leith, husband of Margaret Gladstones, who was born 1763, died 5 May 1814. [North Leith gravestone]

CRUIKSHANKS, JAMES, a surgeon in Edinburgh, married Mary Calder, daughter of William Calder MD, of Edisto Island, South Carolina, in Dean, Bo'ness, West Lothian, on 19 September 1823. [S.388.624]

CRUIKSHANK, PATRICK, from St Vincent, husband of Margaret Davidson, [1748-1779], parents of Catherine Cruikshank who died in 1779. [Greyfriars gravestone, Edinburgh]

CUDDIE, THOMAS, a gardener from Corstorphine, with his wife Marion, emigrated via Greenock to Canada in 1815. [TNA.CO385.2]

CULLEN, THOMAS, of 48 Findhorn Place, Edinburgh, father of Thomas Leslie Cullen, born 1852, died in Melbourne, Victoria, Australia, on 7 June 1884. [S.12801]

CUMMING, WILLIAM, in Jamaica, son and heir of William Cumming, a writer in Edinburgh, in 1802. [NRS.S/H]

CUMMINS, ROBERT, a carver and gilder in Edinburgh, versus his wife Jean Anderson, a Process of Divorce in 1794. [NRS.CC8.5.23]

CUNNINGHAM, ALEXANDER, a Writer to the Signet in Edinburgh, father of Granville Carlyle Cunningham who married Frances Bethune Crooks, youngest daughter of Robert Pilkington Crooks a barrister in Toronto, Ontario, there on 14 August 1873. [EC.27737]

CUNNINGHAME, GEORGE, born 1749, Surveyor General of Customs, died on 9 July 1819, husband of Margaret Corsane, born in 1753, died on 30 April 1842, parents of Margaret Cunninghame who died on 22 June 1823, Edward Cunninghame, of H.M. Customs in Beirut, died in 1850, George Corsane Cunninghame, formerly Customs Collector in Mauritius, born 1788, died on 3 October 1872, and Jane Cunninghame who died on 19 October 1872. [Grayfriars gravestone]

CUNNINGHAM, JAMES, in California, brother and heir of Thomas Cunningham in Edinburgh, in 1859. [NRS.S/H]

CUNNINGHAM, JOHN, born 1779, son of Thomas Cunningham a painter in Edinburgh, died in Dominica in May 1803. [SM.66.566]

CUNYNGHAM, WILLIAM HENRY DICK, born 16 June 1851, Victoria Cross, Lieutenant Colonel of the 2nd Battalion of the Gordon Highlanders, who was mortally wounded at the defence of Ladysmith, Natal, South Africa, and died on 7 January 1900, son of Sir William Cunyngham of Prestonfield. [Duddingston gravestone]

CURRIE, Reverend DAVID, from Edinburgh, emigrated to Virginia around 1730, tutor to the Lee Family, minister of Christ Church in Virginia from 1742 until 1792. [OD]

CUSHNIE, A., a glover and breeches maker, 54 Leith Street, Edinburgh, 1849. [POD]

CUSHNIE, GEORGINA VALLANCE, in Charleston, South Carolina, daughter and heir of Jean Vallance, wife of Alexander Cushnie, a glover in Edinburgh, who died on 26 May 1841; also, sister and heir of Jane Cushnie, wife of George Fisher a comedian in Edinburgh later in New York, who died in November 1856. [NRS.S/H]

CUTHBERTSON, JOHN, born 1802 in Edinburgh, a joiner and a soldier of the 70th Regiment, was imprisoned in Glasgow tolbooth accused of the murder of John Rogers, a prisoner there, in 1820. [NRS.AD14.20.18]

CUTHBERTSON, W. F., 14 Circus Place, Edinburgh, 1849. [POD]

DALLAS, ALEXANDER, mate of the Hibernia of Leith, was drowned in its shipwreck, when bound from St John, New Brunswick, to Liverpool, on 19 January 1810. [NBRG]

DALLAS, ALEXANDER, born 1777, Quartermaster of the 93rd Highlanders, died on 12 January 1856, husband of Jane Chalmers, born 1774, died on 6 August 1843. [Greyfriars gravestone]

DALLAS, GEORGE, son of James Dallas a brewer, was apprenticed to James Christie and Richard Dick, tobacconists in Edinburgh, for six years, on 20 June 1799. [ERA]

DALMAHOY, JOHN CHRISTIE, son of John Dalmahoy, in Jamaica, heir to his grand-uncle Alexander Dalmahoy, a shoemaker in Edinburgh, in 1824; also, heir to his grand-aunt Elizabeth Dalmahoy, widow of Robert Wright, a master mariner in the Royal Navy, in 1824. [NRS.S/H]

DALRYMPLE, INGRAM WILLIAM, son of Martin Dalrymple and his wife Frances Ingram, was born on 16 May 1799 and was baptised in the church of St John the Evangelist, Edinburgh, on 7 June 1799. [NRS.CH12.3.26.7]

DARLING, WILLIAM, stay and corset maker, 94 South Bridge, Edinburgh, 1849. [POD]

DARLING, WILLIAM, born 1797, a merchant from Edinburgh, died in Montreal, Quebec, on 19 January 1871. [East Preston Street cemetery, Edinburgh]

DAVIDSON, BRYCE, postmaster at Lake Opinicon, Ontario, son and heir of Bryce Davidson, a painter in Leith, who died on 18 February 1831. [NRS.SH]

DAVIDSON, JAMES, born 1764, a Major in the Service of the East India Company, died at Portobello on 31 August 1825. [Duddingstone gravestone]

DAVIDSON and GRAY, stone warehousemen and tenants in the Bush, Leith, in 1811. [LD]

DAVIE, ADAM, only son of John Davie of Gavieside and his wfe Mary Flint, a Major in HM Servce, a prisoner of war for nine years in Kandy, Ceylon, died there in July 1812. [Greyfriars gravestone]

DAVIE, ALLAN, a sailor in Leith, husband of Niven Smith, in 1796. [SL.123]

DAWSON, ISABEL, in Pedden's Land, South Leith, was granted a beggar's badge on 18 February 1794. [SLR]

DAWSON, WILLIAM THOMAS, in Philadelphia, Pennsylvania, son and heir of William Dawson, a colour merchant in Leith, who died on 13 September 1854. [NRS.S/H]

DAWSON, WILLIAM, and his wife Harriette Clark, were parents of Elizabeth Harriette Dawson, born 1853, wife of A. Tough, died in Chicago, Illinois, on 15 February 1890. [East Preston gravestone, Edinburgh]

DEAS, JOHN, born 1735 in Leith, son of skipper David Deas and Catherine Dundas, settled in South Carolina in 1749, a Loyalist in 1776, died in Charleston on 30 September 1790, probate 26 November 1790, South Carolina. [TNA.AO12.73.129] [SM.52.517]

DE FLANDRE, M., teacher of Italian, 40 Great King Street, Edinburgh, 1849. [POD]

DENHOLM, EUPHEMIA, daughter of Thomas Denham of General Register House in Edinburgh, married Walter Telfer, a surgeon in Niagara, Upper Canada, in New York on 17 July 1827. [EEC.18089]

DENHOLM, JAMES, born 14 August 1850, son of David Denholm and his wife Janet Steedman, died in Calgary, Canada, on 11 December 1887. [East Preston Street cemetery, Edinburgh]

DENHOLM, WILLIAM, an agricultural implement maker in Mary Place, Edinburgh, 1840. [POD]

DEUCHAR, ROBERT, jr., only son of Robert Deuchar a Solicitor to the Supreme Court, Nicolson Street, Edinburgh, died in Pictou, Nova Scotia, on 11 November 1853. [EEC.22425]

DEUCHAR, ROBERT, only son of Robert Deuchar and his wife Margaret Ritchie, died in Cincinatti, Ohio, on 10 April 1863. [Greyfriars gravestone, Edinburgh]

DEWAR, JOHN, born 1798, an advocate, died on 28 October 1856, husband of Elizabeth Burnet, born 1795, died 8 December 1874. [Greyfriars gravestone]

DEWAR, MARTHA, in Leith Mills, South Leith, was granted a beggar's badge on 18 February 1794. [SLR]

DEWAR, THOMAS, a graduate of Edinburgh University, minister of St Andrew's in Nassau, the Bahamas from 1827 until his death in 1830. [F.7.671]

DEWAR, W., dancing teacher, 59 South Bridge, Edinburgh, 1849. [POD]

DICK, DAVID, second son of Alexander Dick an accountant in Edinburgh, died in Alvarado, Mexico, in November 1825. [EA.6493.111]]

DICK, DAVID, a seaman in Leith, then in America, brother and heir of Jessy Dick in Edinburgh, who died on 14 December 1858; also, heir to his uncle David Dick in St George, East London, in 1861. [NRS.S/H]

DICKINS, BENJAMIN, was accused of bigamy at George Square, Edinburgh in 1849. [NRS.AD14.49.82]

DICKISON, GEORGE, a joiner in Mound City, Illinois, son and heir of Alexander Dickison, a joiner in Dean, Edinburgh, in 1864. [NRS.SH]

DICKSON, DAVID, born 1811, son of Reverend David Dickson, died in Valparaiso, USA, on 10 April 1884. [St Cuthbert's gravestone, Edinburgh]

DICK, ISOBEL, versus her husband John Carr in the Cowgate of Edinburgh, a Process of Divorce in 1822. [NRS.CC8.6.134]

DICKSON, ISOBEL, wife of James Black a merchant in Leith, who married in December 1781, a Process of Divorce in 179-. [NRS.CC8.6.982]

DICKSON, MARION, married Dr Lynch from Barbados, in Edinburgh on 21 October 1800. [SM.62.779]

DICKSON, WILLIAM, deacon of South Leith parish in 1825. [SLR]; a merchant in Leith, a petitioner in 1828; an elder on 1 October 1843. [SLR]

DOBIE, RICHARD, born 1731 in Liberton, Edinburgh, a fur trader and merchant in Canada, died in Montreal, Quebec, on 23 March 1805. [DCB][GM.75.773]

DOBSON, WILLIAM, a brass-founder and gas fitter, 5 Charles Street, Edinburgh, 1849. [POD]

DON, JOHN, born 1771 in Edinburgh, died in Augusta, Georgia, on 10 August 1810. [Augusta Chronicle. 11.8.1810]

DONALDSON, JOHN, a shipmaster in Leith, testament, 1826, Comm. Edinburgh. [NRS.CC8.8.151.41]

DONALDSON, JOHN, a shipmaster in Leith, testament, 1826, Comm. Edinburgh. [NRS]

DOUGHTIE, WILLIAM, born 1848, son of William Doughtie, [1811-1851], and his wife Isabella Dall, [1808-1881], died in Orlando, Florida, in 1883. [New Calton gravestone]

DOUGLAS, AGNES, daughter of Robert Douglas in Portland Place, North Leith, and wife of Thomas Owston in Pittsburgh, Pennsylvania, died there on 2 November 1850. [EEC.22048]

DOUGLAS, ALEXANDER, son of George Douglas a mathematician was apprenticed to George Chalmers, a locksmith in Edinburgh, for six years, on 16 March 1797. [ERA]

DOUGLAS, or SUTHERLAND, AGNES, of New York and Leith, 1866. [NRS.B22.4.90.20]

DOUGLAS, H., a musical instrument maker and music seller, 115 Kirkgate, Edinburgh, 1849. [POD]

DOUGLAS, JAMES, born 1757 in Edinburgh, son of John Douglas, a public official who died on Prince Edward Island on 26 September 1803. [DCB]

DOUGLAS, JAMES, second son of James Douglas an accountant of the Commercial Bank in Edinburgh, died in Paramaribo, Surinam, on 7 November 1874. [S.9785]

DOUGLAS, JOHN, born in Edinburgh, was naturalised in South Carolina on 29 December 1799. S.C.Miscellaneous Records.Q3.270]

DOUGLAS, ROBERT, a sugar planter of Better Hope, Demerara, died at 25 India Street, Edinburgh, on 5 April 1826. [BM.19.766]; testament, 1864,

DOUGLAS, ROBERT, in Portland Place, North Leith, father of Agnes Douglas, who died in Pittsburgh, Pennsylvania, on 2 November 1850, wife of Thomas Owston. [EEC.22048]

DOUGLAS, WILLIAM, a merchant in St Petersburg, Russia, son and heir of William Douglas a merchant in Leith, in 1814. [NRS.S/H]

DOVE, DAVID, master of the Isabella Simpson of Leith, testament, 1814, Comm. Edinburgh. [NRS.CC8.8.140.172]

DOW, ISABELLA GLENDINNING, wife of David Watt in San Francisco, California, daughter and heir of Jane Glendinning, wife of James Dow, a wright in Edinburgh, who died on 18 April 1857, in 1862; later, in Grass Valley, Nevada, sister and heir of Robert Dow, a baker in Edmonston, who died on 4 April 1865. [NRS.S/H]

DOW, Captain ROBERT RAMSAY, master of the brig James of London, son of J. B. Dow in Leith, died in Honduras in 1853. [EEC.22500]

DOW, WILLIAM, a cork sole manufacturer, 2 St Mary's Wynd, Edinburgh, 1849. [POD]

DOWIE, JOHN, son of John Dowie the mate aboard the cutter Prince William Henry was apprenticed to William Douglas, a merchant in Leith for six years on 19 January 1792. [ERA]

DOWNIE, ELIZABETH, youngest daughter of James Downie in Leith, died in Valparaiso, Chile, on 12 March 1869. [S.8059]

DOWNIE, GEORGE HART, born 1828, son of John Mackay Downie, [1806-1867], and his wife Marion Hart, [1801-1865], in Edinburgh, married Agnes Ranken Wilson, daughter of William Wilson in Kilmarnock, Ayrshire, in New York on 25 December 1854, died in Lefroy, Ontario, on 16 May 1867. [EEC.22687] [Grange gravestone]

DOWNIE, JAMES, only son of James Downie from Leith, died in Valparaiso, Chile, on 12 March 1869. [S.8059]

DOWNIE, JAMES, an engineer, married Jane Sinclair, from North Leith, in Valparaiso, Chile, on 6 August 1862. [S.2276]

DOWNS, ALEXANDER, born 1821, son of James Downs, [1760-1845], and his wife Janet Martin, [1773-1838[, died in Canton, Massachusetts, on 18 January 1865. [South Leith gravestone]

DOWNS, ALEXANDER, in Montreal, Quebec, son and heir of Ann Commins, wife of John Downs in Edinburgh, who died on 1 July 1867. [NRS.S/H]

DOWNS, HENRY, in Montreal, Quebec, son and heir of Ann Commins, wife of John Downs in Edinburgh, who died on 1 July 1867. [NRS.S/H]

DOWNS, JAMES, son of James Downs, [1760-1845], and his wife Janet Martin, [1773-1838[, died in Natick, Massachusetts, in 1912. [South Leith gravestone]

DOWNS, JOHN, born 1837, son of James Downs, [1760-1845], and his wife Janet Martin, [1773-1838[, died in Havershill, Massachusetts, on 3 January 1821. [South Leith gravestone]

DRYBURGH, NEIL, Deacon of the Coopers of South Leith, a letter, 1829. [SLR]

DRYDEN, JOHN, a block-maker and tenant in the Bush, Leith, in 1811. [LD]

DRYSDALE, A., warehouseman, 3 High Street, Edinburgh, 1849. [POD]

DRYSDALE, or MACINTOSH, MARGARET, in Toronto, Ontario, daughter and heir of William Drysdale, a watchmaker in Edinburgh, in 1835. [NRS.S/H]

DRYSDALE, THOMAS, a watchmaker in Quebec, son and heir of William Drysdale, a watchmaker in Edinburgh, in 1835. [NRS.S/H]

DRYSDALE, WILLIAM, a watchmaker in Philadelphia, Pennsylvania, son and heir of William Drysdale, a watchmaker in Edinburgh, in 1835. [NRS.S/H]

DUCHE, ESTHER, daughter of Reverend Jacob Duche in Philadelphia, Pennsylvania, wife of Reverend William Hill in New York, died on 27 December 1835, buried here. [New Calton gravestone]

DUFF, Reverend HENRY, minister of the Second Charge in Leith, from 5 March 1844 until his death in 1873. [SLR]

DUFF, WILLIAM L., a Lieutenant Colonel of the 2nd Illinois Regiment of Artillery, died in the US Civil War, 1861-1865. [Old Calton gravestone]

DUMBRECK, CHRISTIAN, second daughter of William Dumbreck in South Coates, Edinburgh, married William Ruan, MD, on Hannah's Rest Estate, St Croix, Danish Virgin Islands, on 16 February 1823. [BM.15.492]

DUMBRECK, W., a medical practitioner, 14 Dublin Street, Edinburgh, 1849. [POD]

DUNCAN, COLIN, a coal merchant on Old Church wharf, Leith, 1849. [POD]

DUNCAN, DAVID, born 1819 in Edinburgh, son of John Duncan, emigrated to America in 1830, an importer in New York, died in New Jersey on 15 June 1891. [ANY]

DUNCAN, JAMES, an insurance broker, and tenant in the Bush, Leith, in 1811. [LD]

DUNCAN, JAMES, an elder of South Leith parish on 1 October 1843. [SLR]

DUNCAN, JOHN, a pipe maker in Crown Street, Edinburgh, 1849. [POD]

DUNCAN, ROBERT, born 1831, eldest son of Thomas Duncan a brush manufacturer in Edinburgh, late of Fales and Duncan merchants in Rio de Janeiro, died there on 16 June 1876. [S.10287]

DUNCAN, WILLIAM BUTLER, born on 17 March 1830 in Edinburgh, son of Alexander Duncan, was educated at Edinburgh University and at Brown University in Rhode Island, a banker and entrepreneur in America, died in New York on 20 June 1912. [ANY]

DUNLOP, ANDREW VANS, MD, born on 8 February 1805, died on 27 February 1880. 'good work in Scotland and India'. [Greyfriars gravestone]

DUNLOP, GEORGE, of 30 Mitchell Street, Leith, father of Archibald Dunlop, born 1821, by 1846 of the accounting department of the Oriental Bank, was the manager in Canton, China, by 1849, died in Hong Kong in October 1851. [WMC.76]

DUNLOP, ROBERT BRUCE ELLIS, born 1844, sixth son of Henry Dunlop of Craigtoun, [1800-1867], and his wife Alexina Rankin, [1806-1872], died in Kingston, Jamaica, in January 1877. [Dean gravestone, Edinburgh]

DUNLOP, WILLIAM, a merchant in Edinburgh, a merchant in Edinburgh, a summons in 1825. [NRS.SC11.5.1825.82]

DUNN, JOHN, son of James Dunn in Edinburgh, died in America on 20 January 1794. [EA.3155.191]

DUN, WILLIAM, in New South Wales, Australia, son of Reverend W. Dun in Canongait, Edinburgh, and grandson of A. Campbell an Excise collector, 1836. [NRS.S/H]

DURHAM, ISABELLA, daughter of Hercules Durham of the East India Company, died in South Hanover Street, Edinburgh, on 20 August 1833, an inventory, 1833. [NRS]

EAGLE, PETER, a live bird dealer in 36 Frederick Street, Edinburgh, in 1849. [POD]

EASTON, JOHN, MD, born 1778, late surgeon of the 15th Hussars, died in Edinburgh on 22 April 1841. [St Cuthbert's gravestone]

ECKFORD, WALTER, a skinner and wool dealer, Silvermills, Edinburgh, 1849. [POD]

EDGAR, MARY, third daughter of Alexander Edgar of Wedderly, Jamaica, married James Henry Archer, MD, of Dublin Castle, Jamaica, at Mary Place, Edinburgh, on 15 October 1822. [BM.7.691]

EDMONSTONE, JAMES, a shipmaster in Leith, testament, 1826, Comm. Edinburgh. [NRS]

EDWARDS, ALEXANDER, born on 11 April 1814 in Edinburgh, a granite importer in New York, died in Brooklyn on 6 June 1871. [ANY]

EDWARDS MARION, in Edinburgh, mother of Thomas Jeoffreys Edwards, an engineer in Java, Dutch East Indies, 1854. [NRS.S/H]

ELDER, HENRY, an engineer from Edinburgh, died in Lima, Peru, on 1 August 1879. [S.11283]

ELDER, ROBERT, born 1849, a compositor from Edinburgh, died in New York on 4 January 1885. [S.12970]

ELLIOT, HENRY ANDERSON, in Oregon, Washington Territory, grandson and heir of William Elliot, a butcher in Edinburgh, who died in July 1811. [NRS.S/H]

ELLIOT, JOHN JEFFREY, in Oregon, Washington Territory, grandson and heir of William Elliot, a butcher in Edinburgh, who died in July 1811. [NRS.S/H]

ELLIOT, RALPH CHARLES, in Oregon, Washington Territory, grandson and heir of William Elliot, a butcher in Edinburgh, who died in July 1811. [NRS.S/H]

ELLWOOD, J., a hatter, 105 High Street, Edinburgh, in 1849. [POD]

EWART, GEORGE GRAHAM, a teacher in Stratford, Ontario, son and heir of Robert Ewart, a saddler in Edinburgh, in 1854. [NRS.S/H]

EWING, Reverend ALEXANDER, son of Alexander Ewing a mathematician in Edinburgh, was educated at Edinburgh University, settled in Bermuda as an Anglican minister in 1787, died in Bermuda on 18 October 1822. [EA.6172.47] [EMA.26] [SM.86.255] [FPA.246]

FAED, JOHN, a miniature painter, 16 Duncan Street, Edinburgh, 1849. [POD]

FAED, THOMAS, an artist in 16 Comely Bank, Edinburgh, in 1849. [POD]

FAIR, THOMAS, a merchant, married Harriott Kendall, in Buenos Ayres, Argentina, on 29 March 1818. [BM.3.628]; later, in Hope Crescent, Edinburgh, father of Thomas Fair jr., born 1823, who was drowned on his father's estate of San Jorge on the Rio Negro, Banda Oriental, on 7 November 1853. [EEC.22540]

FAIRBAIRN, JAMES, son of James Fairbairn a sergeant of the 90th Regiment of Foot, was born on 10 December 1798 and was baptised in the church of St John the Evangelist, Edinburgh, on 16 December 1798. [NRS.CH12.3.26.5]

FAIRBAIRN, JAMES, an engraver in Edinburgh, father of James Fairbairn, born 1851, died in Brisbane, Queensland, Australia, on 6 November 1884. [S.12973]

FAIRFOULL, JOHN, born 1779, a builder in Joppa, died 17 August 1837, husband of Helen Gray, born 1782, died 25 July 1867. [Duddingston g/s]

FAIRHOLM, THOMAS, a merchant in Edinburgh, later in Tobago, testament, 24 February 1791, Comm. Edinburgh. [NRS]

FAIRLEY, J., umbrella maker, 35 Nicolson Street, Edinburgh, 1849. [POD]

FALCONER, ANDREW, born 22 January 1824 in Edinburgh, died in South Africa on 4 October 1906. [St George gravestone, Port Elizabeth, Cape of Good Hope]

FARLEY, SARAH, from Edinburgh, later in Savannah, Georgia, probate, 1844, Prerogative Court of Canterbury. [TNA]

FARQUHAR, ALEXANDER, a tavernkeeper, 46 Shore, Leith, 1849. [POD]

FARQUHARSON, Colonel, married Rebecca Colquhoun, fourth daughter of Sir George Colquhoun of Tillycolquhoun, in St Paul's Chapel, Edinburgh, on 17 December 1819. [SM.85]

FARRELL, Dr JOHN, from New Orleans, Louisiana, died at 48 Great King Street, Edinburgh, on 9 February 1854. [EEC.22540]

FEARNS, WILLIAM, teacher of English, Nicolson Square, Edinburgh, 1849. [POD]

FENWICK, GEORGE, son of George Fenwick a goldsmith in Edinburgh, died in Castara, Tobago, on 4 September 1821. [SM.88.619]

FERENBACH, D., a watchmaker, Nicolson Street, Edinburgh, 1849. [POD]

FERGUSON, C., master of the Rajah of Leith from Leith with passengers bound for Hobart, Tasmania, and Sydney, New South Wales, Australia, on 5 April 1838. [LCL.XXV.2587/2620]

FERGUSON, JOHN, master of the Brothers of Leith, from Leith via Newcastle to Baltimore, Maryland, Philadelphia, Pennsylvania, and Richmond, Virginia, in 1820. [EEC.17000][EA.5895]

FERGUSON, JOHN, from Edinburgh, former apprentice to Muir, Wood and Company, musical instrument makers and music sellers in Edinburgh, in Rio de Janeiro, Brazil in 1822. [NRS.CS17.1.41.319]

FERGUSON, ROBERT, a merchant in Manchester, Jamaica, second son of Thomas Ferguson formerly in Leith, died in Howard House, Detroit, Michigan, on 12 September 1855. [EEC.322800] [NRS.SC70.1.93] [W.XVI.1697]

FERGUSON, ROBERT, a soldier of F Company, 97th Regiment of New York Infantry Volunteers, died during the US Civil War, 1861-1865. [Old Calton gravestone, Edinburgh]

FERGUSON, WILLIAM, of Charlotte Street, Leith, father of William Ferguson, born 1854, was drowned near Vera Cruz, Mexico, on 6 February 1872. [S.9002]

FERME, JOHN, in New York, son and heir of George Ferme in Crichton House, Edinburgh, in 1842. [NRS.S/H]

FERRIER, JOHN PLAIN, in Big Oakflat, California, son and heir of David Ferrier, a bookbinder in Edinburgh, who died on 13 June 1859. [NRS.S/H]

FERRIER, WILLIAM, in Oamaru, New Zealand, son of Catherine Leith Lowe, wife of David Ferrier, in Edinburgh, who died on 15 March 1866. [NRS.S/H]

FIDDES, WILLIAM, spirit dealer, 4 Cowgate, Edinburgh, 1849. [POD]

FIELD, GEORGE, married Mrs Jessie MacLean, widow of John MacLean in Carriacou near Grenada, in Edinburgh in 1822. [DPCA.1026]

FIELD, WILLIAM, son of Dr James Field, a physician in Peterburg, Virginia, was apprenticed for three years under Alexander and Patrick Crichton, coachmakers in Edinburgh, on 2 June 1796. [ERA]

FIFE, WILLIAM, brother of Barclay Fife a merchant in Leith, died in Jamaica on 6 January 1810. [PC.63]

FINDLATOR, ALEXANDER, in Otago, New Zealand, died 1858. [Grayfriars gravestone]

FINDLAY, GEORGE, a skipper in Leith, master of the George and Mary of Leith, testament, 13 June 1796, Comm. Edinburgh. [NRS]

FINLAY, JOHN STEELE, born 1832, third son of John Finlay in Edinburgh, died in Boston, Massachusetts, on 9 July 1884. [S.12805]

FINLAY, ROBERT, born 1782, a writer in Spanish Town, Jamaica, died on 13 January 1817. [Greyfriars gravestone, Edinburgh]

FINDLAY, WILLIAM, a gardener in Rhode Island, son and heir of William Findlay, a gardener in Edinburgh, who died on 21 February 1859. [NRS.S/H]

FINLAYSON, ALEXANDER LOCKHART, son of William Finlayson, Depute Clerk of the Bills in Edinburgh, died in Savannah-la-Mar, Jamaica, on 23 July 1823. [EA][BM.14.6241]

FINLAYSON, DAVID, in Savanna-la-Mar, Jamaica, Member of the Jamaican Assembly for Westmoreland, Jamaica, died in Edinburgh on 3 February 1799. [EA.3663.87] [AJ.2666]

FINLAYSON, GEORGE, a mariner, testament, 1802, Comm. Edinburgh. [NRS]

FINLAYSON, JOHN, youngest son of William Finlayson, Depute Clerk of the Bills in Edinburgh, died in Savannah-la-Mar, Jamaica, in 1800. [GC.1364]

FINLAYSON, MATTHEW, born 1832, a dental surgeon, died on 8 January 1889, his wife Jemima Kay, born 1842, died 22 March 1911. [St Cuthbert's gravestone, Edinburgh]

FINLAYSON, WILLIAM, in Jamaica, third son of William Finlayson, Depute Clerk of the Bills in Edinburgh, died in Edinburgh, on 4 May 1803. [EEC.14260]

FISHER, JAMES WAUCHOPE, on Hampstead Estate, Trelawney, Jamaica, son and heir of Charles Fisher, a solicitor of the Supreme Court in Edinburgh, who died on 4 August 1850. [NRS.S/H]

FLANIGAN, M., a pawnbroker, 142 Cowgate, Edinburgh, 1849. [POD]

FLEMING, BEATRICE, widow of J. Thomson in Georgia, daughter and heir of Margaret Boswell or Fleming in Edinburgh, in 1806. [NRS.S/H]

FLEMING, ELIZABETH, wife of Andrew Joseph Ford in Walcotville, North America, niece and heir of John Barrowman in Edinburgh, who died in October 1850. [NRS.S/H]

FLEMING, HELEN, in Georgia, heir of Margaret Boswell, wife of David Fleming a currier in Edinburgh, in 1806. [NRS.S/H]

FLETCHER, PETER, a globe maker, 19 Rose Street, Edinburgh, 1849. [POD]

FLETT, WILLIAM, a tea and coffee dealer, 10 St Anthony Street, Leith, 1849. [POD]

FORBES, GEORGE, a banker in Edinburgh, died on 26 September 1857, father of Charles William Forbes in Ceylon. [NRS.S/H]

FORBES, HELEN, wife of A. Clark in Norfolk, Virginia, sister and heir of David Forbes, a carver in Edinburgh, in 1815. [NRS.S/H]

FORBES, SOPHIA HORN, third daughter of Alexander Forbes, and wife of James Grant, died in Montreal, Quebec, on 20 November 1858. [St Cuthbert's gravestone, Edinburgh]

FORDYCE, EMILIA, daughter of Alexander Fordyce of the Royal Navy, married Dr John Stennet, MD, of St James, Jamaica, in Edinburgh in 1791. [SM.53.151]; she died in Jamaica in March 1803. [EA.4124.03]

FORGAN, D., wood merchant, Milne's Close, 212 Canongate, Edinburgh, 1849. [POD]

FORREST, JAMES, surgeon in the Royal Navy, died in Lauriston, Edinburgh, on 30 December 1819. [SM.85]

FORREST, JOHN, born 19 September 1799 in Edinburgh, minister of the Old Scots Church in Charleston, South Carolina, for 47 years, died 12 July 1879. [Old Scots gravestone]; was naturalised in South Carolina on 14 December 1840. [NARA.M1183.1]

FORREST,......, son of Adam Forrest a porter, was apprenticed to John Sibbald, a locksmith in Edinburgh, for six years, in 1799. [ERA]

FORRESTER, FRANCIS, born 1746, of the firm Peter and Francis Forrester in Leith, an associate of Charles Cameron the architect, died in St Petersburg, Russia, in 1811. [SSR.10]

FORRESTER, PETER, and FRANCIS FORRESTER, merchants in Leith, in 1793. [NRS.CS97.107.9]

FORSHAW, H., a livery stable keeper, 11 Hill Street Lane, Edinburgh, in 1849. [POD]

FORSYTH, ALEXANDER, a foreman in Thomas Jamieson and Son, soap boilers in Leith, and Thomas Doyle, a soap boiler in Leith, subscribed to a bond ensuring that George Rogers, a soap boiler in Leith, would not harm John Johnston, macer of the Woollen Manufactory in Leith, 1800. [NRS.CS271.1.343]

FORSYTH, ANDREW, a midshipman aboard the East Indiaman Woodford, son of Andrew Forsyth, a skipper in Leith, and his wife Ann Reid, testament, 17 September 1800, Comm. Edinburgh. [NRS]

FORTUNE, GEORGE JAMES, a shipmaster in Leith, testament, 1819, Comm. Edinburgh. [NRS.CC8.8.145.63]

FORTUNE, MATTHEW, died on 19 October 1818, husband of Helen St Ledger Gillies, died 14 September 1834, parents of Lieutenant William Fortune of the 31st Regiment, born 1812, died 26 March 1836. [Greyfriars gravestone]

FORTUNE, ROBERT, a slater, 4 South Junction Street, Edinburgh, 1849. [POD]

FOSTER, RICHARD, born 1755, died in Charles Street, Edinburgh, on 25 August 1822. [SM.90.631]

FOTHERINGHAM, JAMES, a baker of 8 Cannon Street, Leith, in 1849. [POD]

FOWLER, ALEXANDER, a builder in Edinburgh, father of James D. Fowler who died in Montreal, Quebec, on 13 April 1885. [S.13042]

FRAME, LOCKHART, a bookbinder in 13 Bank Street, Edinburgh, in 1849. [POD]

FRANKS, B., an optician, 1 Elm Row, Edinburgh, 1849. [POD]

FRASER, ANDREW, a currier from Edinburgh who emigrated to New York, died in New Orleans, Louisiana, in 1853. [S.21.9.1853]

FRASER, ARCHIBALD, a police watchman in Edinburgh, accused of theft in 1815. [NRS.AD14.15.13]

FRASER, BAILEY SIMPSON, born 1808, lately from New Orleans, Louisiana, died in Portobello, Midlothian, on 16 July 1861. [East Preston gravestone, Edinburgh]

FRASER, CATHERINE, from Edinburgh, emigrated to Canada, marred Alexander Fraser jr, a merchant in Miramachi, New Brunswick, at Chatham Head, NB, on 22 June 1822. [SM]

FRASER, COLIN MACKENZIE, of Register House in Edinburgh, marred Elizabeth Willis, third daughter of Robert Willis of Martha Brae, Jamaica, in London on 4 September 1827. [S.801.5831]

FRASER, DONALD, in Cowfeeder Row, Edinburgh, a victim of theft in 1849. [NRS.AD14.49.118]

FRASER, GEORGE, a hair manufacturer, 51 West Port, Edinburgh, 1849. [POD]

FRASER, JAMES, son of Mr Fraser, a teacher in St James Square, Edinburgh, died in Falmouth, Jamaica, on 6 February 1821. [DPCA] [BM.9.245]

FRASER, JAMES, born 25 January 1826 in Edinburgh, son of Andrew Fraser and his wife Isabella Smith, settled in New York in 1842 as a leather merchant, died on 15 December 1897. [ANY]

FRASER, JOHN, son of James Fraser a carpenter in Leith, was apprenticed to Charles Ritchie, a hardware merchant in Edinburgh, for five years on 7 August 1794. [ERA]

FRASER, JOHN, born 1797, son of Mr Fraser, a teacher in 23 St James Square, Edinburgh, died in Falmouth, Jamaica, on 23 May 1820. [BM.7.583]

FRASER, JOSEPH, born 1780, a copper and iron plate worker, with his wife born 1781, Francis born 1810, Jean born 1813, and John, emigrated from Leith bound for Halifax, Nova Scotia, in 1817. [TNA.CO384.1.116.237]

FRASER, MALCOLM, born 1839, youngest son of Alexander Fraser in Albany Street Lane, Edinburgh, died in Buenos Ayres, Argentina, on 6 September 1878. [EC.29338] [S10990]

FRASER, ROBERT, son of Mr Fraser, a teacher in St James Square, Edinburgh, died in Kingston, Jamaica, on 24 October 1820. [BM.8.708]

FREEMAN, RICHARD, tavern keeper, 5 Shakespeare Square, Edinburgh, 1849. [POD]

FREEMAN, THOMAS GODFREY, eldest son of Thomas J. Freeman of HM Customs in Leith, died in Fray Bentos, Uruguay, on 23 June 1872. [S.9067]

FRENCH, Reverend JOHN, born 9 December 1793, a minister in Edinburgh from 1833, died on 11 January 1858; husband of Jane Innes who died on 19 June 1866. [St Cuthbert's gravestone, Edinburgh]

FRENCH, ROBERT, in Canada, heir to his great grandfather James French, a labourer in East Kirkburn, Edinburgh, who died in 1811, in 1875. [NRS.S/H]

FRISLIN, MARY CATHERINE, born 1797, died in Demerara on 15 January 1815. [Grayfriars gravestone]

FRUISH, ROBERT, a shoemaker in Lambs Court, 40 Giles Street, Leith, 1849. [SLR]

FULLARTON, JOHN, born 1764, the Crown Surveyor of Jamaica, died 13 November 1849, husband of Elizabeth ...., [1782-1833]. [St Cuthbert's gravestone, Edinburgh]

FULLARTON, ROBERT, died at 116 Princes Street, Edinburgh, on 16 November 1819. [SM.85]

FYALL, THOMAS, a shipmaster, 2 Hamburg Place, Leith, 1849. [POD]

FYFE, DAVID, a skipper in Leith, testament, 14 July 1797, Comm. Edinburgh. [NRS]

FYFE, GEORGE, son of George Fyfe, a coppersmith in Leith, was apprenticed to Thomas Ferguson, a coppersmith in Edinburgh, for six years on 11 October 1792. [ERA]

FYFFE, ROBERT, born 1775, son of Barclay Fyffe a merchant in Leith, died in Kingston, Jamaica, on 1 August 1794, buried in Kingston Cathedral. [SM.56.655] [Cathedral gravestone] [GM.64.958] [EA]

FYFFE, WILLIAM, a watchmaker from Edinburgh, was admitted as a burgess of Dunfermline, Fife, on 19 November 1789. [DM]

FYFE, WILLIAM, from London, brother-in-law of Barclay Fyfe a merchant in Leith, died in Jamaica on 6 January 1810. [SM.72.238]

GAIRDNER, JAMES, born 1761 in Edinburgh, married Mary Gordon, emigrated to Charleston, South Carolina, by 1780, a cotton planter in Georgia who died in 1830. [BLG]

GAIRDNER, JAMES, in Georgia, son and heir of Rebecca Penman, widow of Andrew Gairdner, a merchant in Edinburgh, in 1826. [NRS.S/H]

GAIRDNER, JAMES PENMAN, in Shady Grove, Georgia, son and heir of James Gairdner, son of James Gairdner, a merchant in Edinburgh, in 1835. [NRS.S/H]

GAIRDNER, JAMES, in Port Gibson, Mississippi, son and heir of James Gairdner, a Customs Clerk in Edinburgh, who died on 10 January 1836. [NRS.S/H]

GAIRDNER, MEREDITH, son of Dr Ebenezer Gairdner and Mrs Harriet Gairdner in Edinburgh, a physician in the Service of the Hudson Bay Company from 1832 until 1835, died in Hawaii on 26 March 1837. [HBRS.4.344]

GAIRDNER, ROBERT HUNTER, an advocate in Quebec, son and heir of Robert Gairdner, a solicitor in Edinburgh, in 1830. [NRS.S/H]

GALLETLY, JOHN, a Solicitor to the Supreme Court in Edinburgh, father of Alexander John Galletly John, born 1851, died in Guaymas, Mexico, on 10 September 1878. [S.11000]

GALLIE, C., a picture dealer, 1 Blenheim Place, Edinburgh, 1849. [POD]

GARDINER, JOHN, in Leith, a marriage contract with Jessie Cleghorn, 30 July 1841. [NRS.RD29.3.23]

GARDNER, STEPHEN GIBSON, eldest son of ...... Gardner an apothecary in Edinburgh, died in Jamaica in 1817. [S.31.17]

GARKIN, DENNIS, spirit dealer, Newhaven, Mid Lothian, in 1849. [POD]

GARRIOCH, ALEXANDER, a stockbroker, 1 Danube Street, Edinburgh, 1849. [POD]

GAUGAIN, JAMES THOMAS, born 1824 in Edinburgh, eldest son of John James Gaugain, died in Mexico in 1847. [SG.17.1700]

GAVIN, WILLIAM, a shipmaster in Leith, testament, 1824, Comm. Edinburgh. [NRS]

GEDDES, CHARLES, born 1749 in Edinburgh, a watchmaker who died in Halifax, Nova Scotia, on 27 September 1810. [EA.4926][SM.73.317]

GEIKIE, J.S., a hairdresser and perfumer, 35 North Bridge Street, Edinburgh, 1849. [POD]

GELLATLY, ANDREW, an Excise officer in Leith, 1795. [NRS.CS97.111.166]

GELLATLY, J. a copperplate printer, 26 George Street, Edinburgh, 1849. [POD]

GELLATLY, WILLIAM, born 1842, son of John Gellatly an engraver in Edinburgh, died in Santiago, Chile, on 13 May 1869. [S.8059]

GENTLE, ALEXANDER, minister at Alves, married Isabella Bogle, daughter of Lauchlan Bogle in Jamaica, at 27 Castle Street, Edinburgh, on 23 October 1828. [S.918.689]

GENTLE, JOHN, teacher of English, 5 Nicolson Square, Edinburgh, 1849. [POD]

GEORGE, WILLIAM, born 1790, an accountant in Edinburgh, died on 16 October 1850; husband of Charlotte Augusta Campbell, born 1811, died 21 January 1886. [St Cuthbert's gravestone, Edinburgh]

GEORGESON, A., a boot and shoemaker, 34 Leith Street, Edinburgh, 1849. [POD]

GERARD, ALEXANDER, of Rochsoles, born 1810, eldest son of Lieutenant Colonel John Gerard, a Lieutenant of the 70th Regiment, drowned in the River Nile, Egypt, on 12 September 1837. [Duddingstone gravestone]

GEYLOR, PETER, master of the tender Eliza of Leith, testament, 1808, Comm. Edinburgh. [NRS]

GIBB, EUPHEMIA, daughter of Thomas Gibb a merchant in Edinburgh, married William Murray, in Brooklyn, New York, on 13 August 1875. [EEC.22479]

GIBB, JOHN, a gentleman's servant, a thief who was sentenced in Edinburgh to transportation to the colonies for life, in July 1793. [AJ.2380]

GIBB, JOHN, born 1786, son of George Gibb in Leith, died in Jamaica on 24 March 1803. [EEC.14272][EA]

GIBB, HUGH, son of Hugh C. Gibson and his wife Mary Anne Denovan, died in Detroit, Michigan, on 31 May 1898. [South Leith gravestone]

GIBB, JAMES, born 22 June 1761 in Edinburgh, died on 2 October 1834. [Old Scots gravestone, Charleston, S.C.]

GIBSON, JAMES, eldest son of Major James Gibson of the Dunbarton Fencibles, and grandson of James Gibson, a surgeon in Edinburgh, died in Berbice on 7 November 1807. [SM.70.398]

GIBSON, JAMES, born 22 June 1761 in Edinburgh, died in South Carolina on 2 October 1834. [Old Scots gravestone, Charleston]

GIBSON, JOANNA, eldest daughter of John Gibson a plumber in Leith, married Thomas Brown, a merchant in Mexico, in Trinity Villa on 5 July 1831. [PA.101]

GIBSON, JOHN, son of William Gibson, [1757-1835], and his wife Janet Henderson, [1763-1829], settled in America. [Colinton gravestone]

GIBSON, JOHN, a plumber in Leith, father of Joanna Gibson who married Thomas Brown, a merchant in Mexico, at Trinity Villa on 5 July 1831. [PA.101]

GIBSON, MUNGO CAMPBELL, born 9 March 1819, a shipowner in Leith, died 25 January 1890. [South Leith church window]

GIBSON, PETER, son of William Gibson, [1757-1835], and his wife Janet Henderson, [1763-1829], settled in America. [Colinton gravestone]

GIBSON, ROBERT, a surgeon, second son of James Gibson, a surgeon in Edinburgh, died in Jamaica on 11 June 1797. [EEC.372]

GIBSON, ROBERT, a stocking maker in Edinburgh, with Jean his wife and five children, emigrated via Greenock to Canada in 1815. [TNA.CO385.2]

GIBSON, WILLIAM, jr., a merchant in Edinburgh, son of William Gibson a merchant burgess of Dunfermline, Fife, was admitted as a burgess of Dunfermline on 10 September 1810. [DM]

GIBSON, WILLIAM, son of John Gibson a ropemaker in Edinburgh, settled in Australia before 1848. [NRS.S/H]

GILES, ALEXANDER, born 1780 in Edinburgh, son of Arthur Giles and his wife Ann Park, settled in New Orleans, Louisiana, by 1830, died in 1852. [New Calton gravestone]

GILES, ANNE MOIR, born 11 March 1838 in New Orleans, Louisiana, daughter of James Park Giles, [1784-1848], and his wife Ann Potter, [1795-1867], died in Edinburgh on 18 May 1839. [Greyfriars gravestone, Edinburgh]

GILES, GRACE FRASER, born 4 August 1836 in Edinburgh, daughter of James Park Giles, [1784-1848], and his wife Ann Potter, [1795-1867], died in New Orleans, Louisiana, on 11 September 1838. [Greyfriars gravestone, Edinburgh]

GILLESPIE, WILLIAM, eldest son of William Gillespie a merchant in Edinburgh, died in Falmouth, Jamaica, on 23 June 1812. [SM.74.727]

GILLESPIE, WILLIAM, born 1752, harbour master in Leith, died 28 September 1813, his wife Margaret Muir, died on 6 June 1827. [North Leith gravestone]

GILMORE, DAVID, born 1740, formerly a ropemaker in St Petersburg, Russia, died on 12 January 1805. [St Cuthbert's gravestone]

GILMOUR, WILLIAM, a currier, 49 South Back of Canongate, Edinburgh, 1849. [POD]

GIRDWOOD, HUGH, born 1805, son of James Girdwood of Kirkbraehead House, Edinburgh, died at his brother's house in Falmouth, Jamaica, on 10 June 1822. [BM.12.519]

GIRLE, G. H., tanner, 125 High Street, Edinburgh, 1849. [POD]

GLADSTONES, THOMAS, born 1733, a merchant in Leith, died 11 May 809, husband of Helen Nelson, born 1740, died 17 July 1806. [North Leith gravestone]

GLEISH, GEORGE D. H., born 1766 in Roberton, Roxburghshire, died in Charleston, South Carolina, on 22 November 1826. [Old Scots gravestone, Charleston]

GLENDINNING, R., a coach hirer, 56 Bernard Street, Edinburgh, 1849. [POD]

GLOAG, JAMES, mathematics teacher, 11 Duncan Street, Edinburgh, 1849. [POD]

GOALEN, T., wright, Morton Street, Leith, 1849. [POD]

GODDARD, WILLIAM, a merchant in Leith, was appointed by Hugh Blackburn in Boston, Massachusetts, as his factor and attorney in 1807. [NRS.RD3.317.299]

GOODAL, JANET, wife of Matthew Horsburgh, from Edinburgh, in America by 1794. [NRS.CS17.1.1396]

GOODSIR, JAMES TOD, in Edinburgh, father of James Goodsir in Melbourne, Victoria, Australia, 1859. [NRS.S/H]

GORDON, CHARLES, born 1786, a surgeon from Edinburgh, emigrated via Oban, Argyll, aboard the Clarendon of Hull bound for Prince Edward Island in August 1808. [TNA.CO226.23]

GORDON, ELIZA, born 1823 in Jamaica, died on 4 March 1840. [Greyfriars gravestone, Edinburgh]

GORDON, GEORGE, born 1806 in Edinburgh, a baker who emigrated to Philadelphia, Pennsylvania, in November 1828, settled in Charleston, South Carolina, in1829, was naturalised there on 10 October 1834. [NCA]

GORDON, JAMES, settled as a merchant in New York by 1846. [New Calton gravestone, Edinburgh]

GORDON, THOMAS, settled as a merchant in Three Rivers, Canada, by 1846. [New Calton gravestone, Edinburgh]

GOUDIE, GAVIN, a mason, 30 Rose Street, Edinburgh, in 1849. [POD]

GOW, JESSIE GLASS, daughter of James Gow in Edinburgh, married Thomas Sinclair from Leith, in Valparaiso, Chile, on 25 November 1870. [S.8583]

GOWAN, WILLIAM, a merchant in Leith, died in Elsinore, Denmark, on 25 September 1823. [SM.92.640]

GRACIE, WILLIAM, a Notary Public in New York, nephew and heir of Mary Gracie or Morison in Virginia then in Edinburgh, in 1830. [NRS.S/H]

GRAHAM, BUCHANAN, son of Robert Graham, MD, Professor of Botany at Edinburgh University, died in Calloa, Peru, on 29 March 1869. [S.8050]

GRAHAM, HUGH, in Upper Canada, son and heir of Hugh Graham in Antigua, later in Edinburgh, 1846. [NRS.S/H]

GRAHAME, JEFFREY, third son of ...... Grahame of 29 Ann Street, Edinburgh, died at Fort Vancouver, British Columbia, on 9 January 1860. [DC.23481] [W.21.2173]

GRAHAM, JEMIMA CHARLOTTE, third daughter of Lieutenant Colonel Graham of the Scots Brigade, married Francis Graham from Jamaica, in Edinburgh Castle on 25 February 1813. [EA.5130.13]

GRAHAM, PETER, son of Peter Graham in Bristo Street, Edinburgh, was apprenticed to William Fraser, a tailor in Edinburgh, for five years on 29 November 1800. [ERA]

GRAHAM, ROBERT, born 1781, a merchant in Kingston, Jamaica, died in Edinburgh on 26 January 1844. [St Cuthbert's gravestone]

GRAINGER, THOMAS, an engineer, 119 George Street, Edinburgh, 1849. [POD]

GRANDISON, W., a steel punch cutter, Croft-an-Righ, Edinburgh, 1849. [POD]

GRANT, ALEXANDER, owner of the Farne of Leith, a bond of caution in 1800. [NRS.AC14.1081]

GRANT, ALEXANDER, in Edinburgh, a Captain in the Service of the East India Company, died on 13 August 1835, an inventory, 1835. [NRS]

GRANT, EMILIA, in Charleston, South Carolina, grand-daughter and heir of William Pillans, a skipper in Leith, in 1796; Emily Grant, daughter of H. Grant the US Consul in London, grand-daughter of William Pillans in Leith, in 1802. [NRS.S/H]

GRANT, GEORGE MORRISON, born 30 December 1815, an assistant surgeon in the Service of the East India Company, was killed near Kabul, Afghanistan, on 13 November 1841. [St Cuthbert's gravestone, Edinburgh]

GRANT, HARRY, son of Robert Grant in Leith, a merchant in Charleston, South Carolina, a deed 1792. [NRS.RD4.252.1272]; heir to his daughters Elizabeth Grant and Emily Grant in 1804. [NRS.S/M]

GRANT, JOHN, in Muckle's Close, South Leith, was granted a beggar's badge on 18 February 1794. [SLR]

GRANT, JOHN, in Leith, a letter from his son in Baltimore, Maryland, re Highland emigration, dated 1803. [NRS.GD248.box 702, bundle 5]

GRANT, MARY JOANNA, only daughter of William Grant in Demerara, married Robert Tulloch of Golden Square, Edinburgh, in 1811. [SM.73.398]

GRANT, PATRICK, born 25 July 1777, fifth son of John Grant a merchant in Leith, settled in Boston, Massachusetts in 1802, married Anna Powell in 1807, drowned in the wreck of the Esther when bound for Baltimore, Maryland, on 20 November 1812. [AJ.3409] [EA.5150.13]

GRANT, ROBERT, a wine merchant in Leith, father of Harry Grant a merchant in Charleston, South Carolina, a deed in 1792. [NRS.RD4.252.1272], and, also, Henry Grant his eldest son in Virginia in 1812. [NRS.CS17.1.31/336]

GRAY, ANDREW, born 1801 in Edinburgh, a gardener in Charleston, South Carolina, was naturalised there on 21 April 1845. [NARA.M1183.1]

GRAY, ANNE, daughter of David Gray in Edinburgh, married William Young from Blantford, Canada West, in Buffalo, New York, on 24 November 1859. [CM.21620]

GRAY, DAVID, second son of James Gray a watchmaker in Edinburgh, died in Grenada on 18 July 1810. [DPCA][EA.4887.279]

GRAY, DAVID, formerly a clerk with the British Linen Company Bank in Edinburgh, later in New York, a bond and disposition of his trustees over a dwelling house in Edinburgh in 1845. [NRS.GD81]

GRAY, JAMES, born 1776 in Edinburgh, third son of David Gray and his wife Anne Somerville, settled in Jamaica, later in Philadelphia, Pennsylvania, died in 1838. [BAF]

GRAY, JAMES B., second son of ..... Gray, a solicitor in Hanover Street, Edinburgh, died in Coldstream, on 20 October 1819. [EA.5856.33]

GRAY, JAMES, a writer in Edinburgh, brother and heir of William Gray the Customs Controller in Montserrat, in 1794. [NRS.S/H]

GRAY, JAMES, in Buffalo, New York, grandson and heir of David Gray, a merchant in the Grassmarket, Edinburgh, who died in 1800. [NRS.S/H]

GRAY, JAMES, and his wife Christina......, of 2 Broughton Place, Edinburgh, were parents of William Gray who died in Rio de Janeiro, Brazil on 12 April 1879. [S.11184]

GRAY, JOHN WILLIAM, in Tuchahoe, USA, nephew and heir of William Gray, a merchant in Leith, also, to his father Andrew Gray in Tuchahoe, in 1847. [NRS.S/H]

GRAY, JOHN, 'Auld Jock, master of "Greyfriars Bobby"', died in 1858. [Greyfriars gravestone]

GRAY, WILLIAM, a merchant, married Louise Mackay, only daughter of Lewis Mackay of Kingston, Jamaica, in Edinburgh on 18 December 1820. [EA.5955.391]

GRAY, WILLIAM D., from Edinburgh, a resident of Buffalo, New York, married Henrietta A. Perry, eldest daughter of Miles Perry in Auburn, New York, there on 30 November 1859. [CM.21620]

GREENSHIELDS, in Melbourne, Victoria, Australia, possibly from Edinburgh, 1856. [NRS.S/H]

GREENSLADE, A., a ladies boot and shoemaker, 52 George Street, Edinburgh, 1849. [POD]

GREGORY, GEORGE, a merchant from Edinburgh who died in Kingston, Jamaica, on 25 May 1822. [DPCA][BM.12.250]

GREIG, DAVID, born 21 November 1810, eldest son of Alexander Greig, [1776-1857], a Writer to the Signet, and his wife Jane Whittet, [1785-1862], an attorney and solicitor in New York who died there on 10 September 1847. [St Cuthbert's gravestone, Edinburgh]

GREIG, JAMES, born 1767 in Edinburgh, a baker and confectioner in New York from 1796 until his death on 20 December 1804. [ANY]

GREIG, JOHN, a gunner in the Royal Navy, son and heir of James Greig of Greighall, Edinburgh, in 1793. [NRS.S/H]

GREIG, JOHN WHITTET, born 11 September 1813, eldest son of Alexander Greig, [1776-1857], a Writer to the Signet, and his wife Jane Whittet, [1785-1862], died in New Orleans, Louisiana, on 17 January 1848. [St Cuthbert's gravestone, Edinburgh]

GREVILLE, R. K., a landscape painter, 33 George Street, Edinburgh, 1849. [POD]

GRIEVE, GIDEON, a merchant in Edinburgh, father of Robert Grieve, a storekeeper, who died in Blue Spur, Tuapeka, New Zealand, on 20 September 1884. [S.12907]

GRIEVE, MARGARET, widow of Reverend Walter Turnbull in Jamaica, heir to her father James Mason, a mason in Edinburgh, who died on 6 June 1847. [NRS.S/H]

GRIEVE, WALTER, elder of South Leith parish in 1825. [SLR]; a merchant in Leith, later in Edinburgh, a petitioner in 1828. [SLR]

GRIEVE, WILLIAM, son of John Grieve, overseer to James Rocheid of Inverleith, was apprenticed to Thomas and David Edward on 4 August 1808. [SM.70.798]

GRINLAY, JOHN, born 1784, eldest son of William Grinlay a broker in Leith, a merchant who died in Charlottetown, Prince Edward Island, Canada, on 4 August 1808. [SM.70.798]

GRINDLAY, THOMAS, elder of South Leith parish in 1825. [SLR]; a merchant in Leith, a petitioner in 1828. [SLR]

GRINLAY, WILLIAM, a broker in Leith, versus David Paterson, an insurance broker in Edinburgh, re insurance on the Hopewell from Honduras to Leith, 17 July 1795. [NRS.AC7.67]

GRINLAY, WILLIAM, elder of South Leith parish in 1825. [SLR]

GUTHRIE, JOHN, weaver, 6 Heriot Bridge, Edinburgh, 1849. [POD]

GUTHRIE, R., a leather merchant, 61 St Andrew Street, Leith, in 1849. [POD]

HADAWAY, JOHN, baillie of St Anthony's and St James Chapel, Leith, in 1793. [SLR]

HALDANE, ROBERT, possibly from Edinburgh, settled in Bogata, Columbia, before 1840. [NRS.S/H]

HALL, ROBERT, a police watchman in Edinburgh, accused of theft in 1815. [NRS.AD14.15.13]

HALL, ROBERT, born 13 July 1826 in Edinburgh, a merchant in New York, died on 28 March 1889. [ANY]

HALL, WILLIAM, a sailor in Leith, testament, 1806, Comm. Edinburgh. [NRS]

HAMILTON, JAMES, Deacon of the Fleshers of South Leith, a letter, 1829. [SLR]

HAMILTON, MARY ANN, a widow from Edinburgh, married Edward Marshall alias Peter Fisher, a bachelor in the Anglican Cathedral of St John the Baptist, in St John, Newfoundland, on 23 February 1815. [GM.3182]

HAMILTON, THOMAS, the younger, an architect in Edinburgh, was admitted as a burgess and guilds-brother of Ayr, on 6 May 1824. [ABR]

HANDYSIDE, ANDREW, a merchant in Edinburgh, versus his wife Isabella Pender, a Process of Divorce in 1809. [NRS.CC8.5.30]

HARDY, DUNCAN, a shipmaster in Leith, testament, 1824, Comm. Edinburgh. [NRS.CC8.8.150.170]

HARDIE, HANNAH, in Horse Wynd, South Leith, was granted a beggar's badge on 18 February 1794. [SLR]

HARDIE, HENRY, born 1767, son of James Hardie, [1720-1802], a merchant in Quebec who died on 20 August 1805. [Gogar gravestone, Edinburgh]

HARDIE, JAMES, the elder, a merchant in Leith, and his spouse Janet Aire, a sasine, 18 November 1806. [ECA]

HARDY, JAMES, master of the Hibernia of Leith, was drowned in its shipwreck, when bound from St John, New Brunswick, to Liverpool, on 19 January 1810. [NBRG.26.2.1810]

HARDIE, THOMAS, deacon of South Leith parish in 1825. [SLR]; a merchant in Leith, a petitioner in 1828; an elder on 1 October 1843. [SLR]

HARDY, WILLIAM, born 23 May 1785 in Edinburgh, son of Reverend Thomas Hardy and his wife Agnes Young, a Captain in the Service of the East India Company, died in 1824. [F.1.147]

HARDIE, WILLIAM FORRESTER, born 1 June 1833, died in Portland, Maine, on 26 April 1896. [Canongait gravestone]

HARLOW, A., a nail manufacturer, 31 Commercial Street, Edinburgh, 1849. [POD]

HARPER, ROBERT, a saddler and harness maker, 13 West Maitland Street, Edinburgh, 1849. [POD]

HARRIS, ANDREW, a pocket-book maker, 45 Princes Street, Edinburgh, 1849. [POD]

HARRIS, or MILLER, ANN, in Portsmouth, USA, niece and heir to Agnes Miller, widow of John Thomson, a skipper in Leith, in 1830. [NRS.S/H]

HARRIS, ELIZABETH ANN, versus her husband Andrew Ramsay a slater in Edinburgh, 1804. [NRS.CC8.5.28]

HARRIS, HELEN CAROLINE, daughter of Dr Thomas R. Harris in Philadelphia, Pennsylvania, died in Edinburgh on 7 February 1811. [SM.73.238]

HART, ANNE ELIZABETH, only daughter of William Hart in Madras, India, married Langford Lovell Hodge from Antigua, in Edinburgh on 2 April 1830. [BM.27.964]

HARTHILL, JOHN, born 1780, a publisher in Edinburgh, died 8 May 1865; husband of Mary Watt, born 1793, died on 7 February 1877. [St Cuthbert's gravestone]

HAY, JESSIE, daughter of William Hay, a surgeon in New York, married William Smith in Edinburgh on 21 December 1820. [S.211.39]

HERDMAN, ANDREW, a teacher, died on 7 April 1861, husband of Isobel Miller, who died on 19 January 1882. [St Cuthbert's gravestone, Edinburgh]

HAY, CHRISTIAN, in Heriot Row, Edinburgh, died 18 August 1842, relict of George Hardyman a Lieutenant Colonel of the East India Company, an inventory, 1842. [NRS]

HAY, ISABELLA, in St Andrew Square, Edinburgh, died on 31 May 1826, relict of John Forbes a Major General of the East India Company, an inventory, 1827. [NRS]

HAY, JEAN, born 1792, daughter of Alexander Hay, a brush manufacturer, and his wife Ann Tuck, died in Canada in 1864. [Canongait gravestone]

HAY, JAMES, was born in the East Indies in December 1795 and baptised in the church of St John the Evangelist in Edinburgh on 29 January 1799. [NRS.CH12.3.26.5]

HAY, JOHN, born 1817, son of Peter Hay, [1786-1837], a merchant in Edinburgh, and his wife Alison Bathgate, [1795-1853], died in Natchez, Mississippi, in 1844. [New Calton gravestone]

HEDGE, LOUISA, wife of Reverend Henry Wilkes late of the Albany Street Chapel in Edinburgh, died in Montreal, Quebec, on 8 September 1838. [SG.7.708]

HEDRICH, FRANZ, born 30 July 1823 in Prague, an author and poet, died 31 October 1895. [Greyfriars gravestone]

HEITELIE, WILLIAM, born 1783, from Duncliffe, Edinburgh, died in Dunedin Park, Mosa, Canada West, on 9 February 1855. [EEC.22719]

HENDERSON, ANDREW, a haberdasher in Leith, from 1795 to 1796. [NRS.CS96.2043.1-2]

HENDERSON, ANN, relict of Alexander Henderson a merchant, died in Leith on 25 November 1822. [SM.90.632]

HENDERSON, BALFOUR, a planter in Jamaica, brother and heir of Daniel Henderson, a writer in Edinburgh, in 1820. [NRS.S/H]

HENDERSON, DAVID, born 1785, a surgeon in the Service of the East India Company, died in Edinburgh on 3 January 1832. [St Cuthbert's gravestone]

HENDERSON, JAMES, from Edinburgh, died in Buenos Ayres, Argentina, on 3 December 1871. [S.8861]

HENDERSON, JOHN, born 1784, a builder in Stafford Street, Edinburgh, died in 1860, husband of Margaret Spence, born 1782, died 1822, parents of Walter Henderson, born in March 1844, died in San Francisco, California, in May 1884. [St Cuthbert's gravestone]

HENDERSON, PATRICK, in New South Wales, Australia, son of Alison Johnston or Henderson in Edinburgh, 1850. [NRS.S/H]

HENDERSON, PETER, in St John, Newfoundland, a sasine, 17 November 1820. [NRS.RS.Edinburgh.17.19]

HENDERSON, THOMAS, born 1812, of Duddingston Mills, died 26 February 1871, husband of Margaret Spink, born 1812, died 6 April 1882. [Duddington gravestone]

HENDERSON, WALTER, born in March 1844, son of John Henderson, died in San Francisco, California, in May 1884. [St Cuthbert's gravestone, Edinburgh]

HENDERSON, WILLIAM, deacon of South Leith parish in 1825. [SLR]

HENDRIE, J., a tobacconist, 2 Baker's Place, Edinburgh, 1849. [POD]

HENDRIE, KINLOCH, son of Alexander Hendrie a merchant in Edinburgh, died in Dominica on 13 March 1807. [SM.69.477]

HENNING, WILLIAM, son of William Henning and his wife Margaret, was born on 24 April 1798 and was baptised in the church of St John the Evangelist in Edinburgh on 9 May 1798. [NRS.CH12.3.26.3]

HENRY, ISABELLA, daughter of Captain Henry in Leith, married John Thomson, a merchant, in Quebec on 27 September 1823. [S.404.752]

HENRY, JOHN C., a printer from Edinburgh, father of a son born at Cove, St Stephen's, New Brunswick, on 15 April 1873. [EC.27634]

HENRY, J., an artificial limb maker at 3 Infirmary Street, Edinburgh, in 1849. [POD]

HENRY, MARGARET MARY, born 9 February 1854 in New Brunswick, daughter of George Henry, died in Edinburgh on 19 November 1857. [St Cuthbert's gravestone, Edinburgh]

HEPBURN, P., son of Thomas Hepburn a merchant in Edinburgh, died on St Vincent in 1795. [SM.57.480]

HEWAT, RICHARD, in Australia, then in Toronto, Ontario, grandson and heir of Margaret Walker, widow of A. MacEwan, a bootmaker in Edinburgh, in 1864. [NRS.S/H]

HILDITCH, SAMUEL GEORGE, born 1848, son of Samuel Hilditch in Edinburgh, died in Montreal, Quebec, on 18 March 1873. [EC.27619]

HILL, ESTHER DUCHE, daughter of Reverend Jacob Duche in Philadelphia, Pennsylvania, and relict of Reverend William Hill in New York, died on 27 December 1835. [New Calton gravestone, Edinburgh]

HILL, JAMES, a coach hirer in Leith, 1791-1792. [NRS.CS96.3332]

HILL, JOHN, master of the Ossian of Leith bound from Inverness to Pictou, Nova Scotia, in 1821. [NRS.E504.17.9]

HILL, PETER, jr., son of Peter Hill a cess collector in Edinburgh, married Ann MacDowell, only daughter of Daniel MacDowell of St Vincent, in Edinburgh on 16 August 1824. [DPCA.1152]; he died on St Vincent on 9 November 1829. [SM.27.968]

HILL, ROBERT, son of Peter Hill, a cess collector in Edinburgh, died in Jamaica in May 1827. [BM.22.58]

HILL, Reverend T., from Edinburgh, emigrated to Canada in 1823, died in Montreal, Quebec, on 14 March 1824. [EA]

HODGE, ROBERT, born 1746 in Edinburgh, emigrated via London to Philadelphia, Pennsylvania, in 1770, a bookseller in New York, died on 23 August 1813. [ANY]

HOFFMAN, J. R., a plane maker in Lothian Street, Edinburgh, 1849. [POD]

HOGG, GRACE, wife of Thomas Sutherland, from Edinburgh, died at Sutherland Moor, River St Clair, Canada West, in 1853. [S.16.7.1853]

HOGG, Dr ROBERT, a surgeon in Edinburgh, died in New York on 1 June 1830. [BM.28.573]

HOLMES, ALEXANDER, born 9 May 1789 in Edinburgh, editor of the 'Cornwall Chronicle', died at Montego Bay, Jamaica, on 18 September 1861. [Montego Bay gravestone]

HOLYWELL, JESSIE, wife of David Palmer, a meal dealer in Edinburgh, brother and heir of John Holywell, an engineer in Dunbar later in New York, who died on 25 August 1849. [NRS.S/H]

HOME, Sir GEORGE, of Blackadder, born 1740, a Vice Admiral of the Blue, died on 2 May 1803. [Greyfriars gravestone]

HOME, JAMES, of Linhouse, a Writer to the Signet, Clerk of Session, and Deputy Lord Lyon, died on 2 January 1819, husband of

HONYMAN, WILLIAM THOMSON, of Mansfield, died in Naples, Italy, on 25 August 1828, husband of Catherine Thomson, who died on 15 June 1832. [St Cuthbert's gravestone, Edinburgh]

HOPE, WILLIAM, born 26 December 1788, died 29 January 1846, husband of Mary Park, born 10 June 1806, died 10 September 1881. [Duddingston gravestone]

HOPKIRK, THOMAS, a grocer and spirit dealer, 25 Charles Street, Edinburgh, 1849. [POD]

HOPPERTON, SAMUEL, a coal merchant, 6 West Preston Street, Edinburgh, 1849. [POD]

HORNER, JOHN, born 1751, a merchant, died in 1829, husband of Joanna Baillie, born 1755, died in 1827. [St John's gravestone, Edinburgh]

HORSBURGH, S., an engraver, 18 Buccleugh Place, Edinburgh, 1849. [POD]

HORSBURGH, THOMAS, born 1800, died 27 July 1854; husband of Jane Rae, born 1790, died 25 February 1865. [St Cuthbert's gravestone]

HORSMAN, WILLIAM, born 1758, died 1845, his first wife Jane ..., born 1770, died in 1733, his second wife Mary Turner, died in 1841. [St John's gravestone, Edinburgh]

HOUSTON, E. N., a medical practitioner, 15 Union Street, Edinburgh, 1849. [POD]

HOWDEN, WILLIAM, son of Matthew Howden and his wife Ann Beath, a chemist who died in San Francisco, California, in 18... [New Calton gravestone, Edinburgh]

HOWELL, JOHN, a polyartist, 110 Rose Street, Edinburgh, 1849. [POD]

HUGHES, JOHN, born 1811 in County Monaghan, Ireland, a labourer in Blackfriar's Wynd, Edinburgh, was accused of arson in 1849. [NRS.AD14.49.100]

HUME, ALEXANDER, innkeeper at Gibbet Toll, Edinburgh, in 1849. [POD]

HUNT, PETER, born 1809 in County Cavan, Ireland, a coal porter in Todrick's Wynd, Edinburgh, was accused of arson in 1849. [NRS.AD14.49.100]

HUNTER, GEORGE, born 1783, Lieutenant Colonel of the 23rd Regiment of Native Infantry on the Madras Establishment of the East India Company, died on 2 April 1832. [Greyfriars gravestone]

HUNTER, Mrs MARGARET, in Granton, Midlothian, widow of Walter Miller, a merchant in Jamaica, 18 December 1847. [NRS.SC70.1.77]

HUNTER, PATRICK, in Edinburgh, formerly a Captain in the Service of the East India Company, died 29 August 1826, an inventory 1827. [NRS]

HUNTER, ROBERT, grandson of Professor Hunter of Edinburgh University, died in Jamaica on 1 January 1805. [SM.67.236]

HUNTER, WILLIAM, son of James Hunter in Richmond Street, Edinburgh, was apprenticed to John More, a painter in Edinburgh, for six years on 31 March 1791. [ERA]

HUTCHEON, JOHN, from Edinburgh, then in New York, son and heir of David Hutcheon, a fisherman in Edinburgh, who died on 20 August 1850. [NRS.S/H]

HUTCHISON, J., master of the Manchester of Leith trading between Leith and Halifax, Nova Scotia, in 1820. [NRS.E504.22.89]

HUTCHISON, THOMAS, born 1796 in Kinghorn, a wine merchant in Leith, Provost there from 1845 to 1848, died 1852, husband of Jane Wylie, born 1805, died 1889. [South Leith church window]

HUTCHISON, ..., a wood merchant and tenant in the Bush, Leith, in 1811. [LD]

HUTTON, GRIZEL, in Leith Mills, South Leith, was granted a beggar's badge on 18 February 1794. [SLR]

HUTTON, JAMES, son of John Hutton, [1798-1871] and his wife Euphemia Dunn, [1825-1875], an engineer aboard the SS Rio de Janeiro, died in Rio de Janeiro, Brazil, on 16 March 1876. [East Preston Street, Cemetery, Edinburgh]

HUTTON, Miss, daughter of William Hutton in Leith, married James Andrew of Craigend, on 15 December 1819. [SM.85]

IMLACH, F. B., a dentist, 55 Queen Street, Edinburgh, 1849. [POD]

IMLACH, GEORGE, a surgeon, born in India on 21 October 1792, son of Colonel Henry Imlach, died in Edinburgh on 8 September 1827. [Greyfriars gravestone]

IMRIE, ELIZABETH, daughter of James Imrie, a writer in Edinburgh, and his wife Elizabeth Bruce, wife of Robert Waterston in Sydney, New South Wales, Australia, 1856. [NRS.S/H]

INGLIS, ANN, born 1834, a housekeeper in Leith, arrived in Hobart, Tasmania, Australia, aboard the Duke of Lancaster on 14 February 1855. [SRA.TD292]

INGLIS, GEORGE, a horse dealer, 10 Rose Street, Edinburgh, in 1849. [POD]

INGLIS, JOHN, born 1805, son of William Inglis, [1775-1833], an Excise Supervisor in Teviotdale, and his wife Jane Tweedie, [1771-1850], a surgeon who died in New York in 1849. [Greyfriars gravestone, Edinburgh]

INNES, GEORGE, a Customs Inspector in New York, brother and heir of Margaret Innes, daughter of George Innes a wright in Edinburgh, 1827. [NRS.S/H]

INVERARITY, JAMES, son of David Inverarity, a cabinetmaker in Canal Street, Edinburgh, was apprenticed to Charles Ritchie, a hardware merchant in Edinburgh, for five years, on 25 October 1792. [ERA]

IRELAND, Reverend WALTER FOGGO, in North Leith, died in February 1828, father of George Ireland in the Service of the East India Company. [NRS.S/H]

IRELAND, JAMES, born 1803 in Edinburgh, died in Geneva, Ontario County, New York, on 2 July 1826. [S.689.519]

IRVINE, CHARLES, in Tobago, died on 11 April 1799. [Greyfriars gravestone, Edinburgh]

IRVINE, CHARLES WILLIAM, youngest son of John Irvine of the Chancery in Edinburgh, died in Tobago on 31 January 1810. [SM.72.317]

IRVINE, JAMES, and his wife Ann ...., in Quebec, parents of James born 1819, died in Edinburgh on 1 October 1820. [Greyfriars gravestone, Edinburgh]

IRVINE, ROBERT, [1800-1860], and his wife Helen Loudoun, [1807-1867], parents of Malcolm Irvine who died in New York. [Grange gravestone, Edinburgh]

IRVINE, THOMAS, born 1802, an auctioneer in Edinburgh, died on 22 June 1850; husband of Elizabeth Mason, born 1794, died 17 February 1863. [St Cuthbert's gravestone]

IRVINE, WILLIAM, in Jamaica, nephew and heir to Andrew Irvine in Edinburgh, in 1806. [NRS.S/H]

ISLES, ANDREW, a leather merchant, 101 Pleasance, Edinburgh, 1849. [POD]

JACK, ARCHIBALD HAY, eldest son of Andrew Jack a printer in Edinburgh, died in Melbourne, Victoria, Australia, on 21 November 1879. [S.11386]

JACK, JEAN, a midwife in Leith, and her husband James Begg in 1796, blackmailers. [NRS.CC8.5.24]

JACKSON, Mrs MARY, born in April 1717 in St Kitt's, wife of Charles Jackson MD, [1728-1785], died in Edinburgh on 9 October 1799. [Greyfriars gravestone, Edinburgh]

JACKSON, ROBERT WINCHESTER, born 28 December 1847 in Leith, son of Robert Lindsay and his wife Agnes Todd, was educated at Edinburgh University, a minister in New Zealand from 1900 to 1921. [F.7.603]

JAFFREY, JAMES, born 1803, a bookseller from Berwick-on-Tweed, died in Galt, Ontario, on 20 October 1884. [S.12901]

JAMES, MARGARET, in Jamaica, heir to her father William John James, an attorney in Jamaica, in 1823,and to her great grand-uncle David Mackie, a merchant in Edinburgh, also, heir to her great grandmother Marion Mackie, wife of W. Mein, a merchant in Edinburgh, in 1826. [NRS.S/H]

JAMES, SUSANNA, second daughter of Hugh James, MD, in Jamaica, and wife of Captain Thomas Phipps Howard of the York Hussars, died in Edinburgh on 10 April 1803. [EEC.14248]

JAMES, WILLIAM JOHN, in Kingston, Jamaica, nephew and heir of Andrew Mein, a merchant in Edinburgh, in 1815. [NRS.S/H]

JAMESON, JANE, second daughter of Robert Jameson a Writer to the Signet, married Walter Skerret Morson, MD, from Montserrat, in Edinburgh on 25 October 1822. [S.302.348]; their second son, Richard Willock Morson, died in Antigua on 17 September 1823. [BM.15.131]

JAMIESON, CATHERINE, born 1820, daughter of George Jamieson and his wife Isabella George, died on Long Island, New York, on 22 December 1851. [East Preston Street gravestone, Edinburgh]

JAMIESON, COLIN, son of Reverend Dr Jamieson in Edinburgh, an Ensign of the 56th Regiment, died in Bellary, Madras, India, on 2 January 1813. [SM.75.959]

JAMIESON, J. and R., merchants, tenants in the Bush, Leith, in 1811. [LD], died there on 23 June 1873. [S.9385]

JAMIESON, WILLIAM, MD, born in Edinburgh, Professor of Botany and Chemistry at the University of Quito, Ecuador, died there on 23 June 1873. [S.9385]

JARDINE, F., teacher at the Sessional School, 249 Canongate, Edinburgh, 1849. [POD]

JARRET, JAMES, a shipmaster in Leith, testament, 1824 Comm. Edinburgh. [NRS.CC8.8.144.57]

JEFFREY, JAMES, born 1837, son of John Jeffrey and his wife Euphemia Hart, died in Shanghai, China, on 17 October 1870. [St Cuthbert's gravestone]

JEFFREY, ROBERT, a copperplate printer, 72 Northumberland Street, Edinburgh, 1849. [POD]

JEFFREYS, THOMAS, a farmer in Edinburgh, with Isabella, his wife, and one child, emigrated via Greenock to Canada in 1815. [TNA.CO385.2]

JENKIESON, ROBERT, a printer in Cincinatti, Ohio, grandson and heir of Robert Jenkieson in Edinburgh, in 1858. [NRS.S/H]

JENKINSON, JOHN, a florist in Philadelphia, Pennsylvania, son and heir of John Jenkinson, a contractor in Leith, who died on 23 May 1861. [NRS.S/H]

JOHNSON, ROBERT, eldest son of Joseph Johnson, a writer in Edinburgh, died in Jamaica in 1817. [S.4.17]

JOHNSON, SAMUEL, born 1787 in Edinburgh, died in Georgia on 13 September 1820. [CMSA.6.8.1820]

JOHNSTON, ANDREW, a confectioner in America, son and heir of George Johnston, a hotel-keeper in Edinburgh, in 1860. [NRS.S/H]

JOHNSTON, GEORGE, in Philadelphia, Pennsylvania, brother and heir of Grace Johnston, wife of James Yates, a gentleman's servant in Edinburgh, in 1825. [NRS.S/H]

JOHNSTON, GEORGE RICHARDSON, born 1848, son of Charles James Johnston in Edinburgh, died at his house in the Camps of Sante Fe, Rosario, Argentina, on 30 December 1873. [Greyfriars gravestone] [EC.27899] [S.9539]

JOHNSTON, HENRY, MD, an assistant surgeon in the Service of the East India Company, Bombay Establishment, at Bushire on the Persian Gulf, died on 16 November 1850. [Greyfriars gravestone]

JOHNSTON, H. J., an elder of South Leith parish on 1 October 1843. [SLR]

JOHNSTON, JAMES, son of John Johnston, a wright in Nicolson Street, Edinburgh, was apprenticed to Alexander Thomson, a confectioner and grocer in Edinburgh, for five years on 16 March 1797. [ERA]

JOHNSTONE, JAMES, of George Square, Edinburgh, in the Service of the East India Company, died 2 February 1837, an inventory, 1837. [NRS]

JOHNSTON, JAMES, a surgeon in Newfoundland, heir to James Johnston, a spirit dealer in Edinburgh, who died in June 1850. [NRS.S/H]

JOHNSTON, JAMES, a meal dealer in Edinburgh, and his wife Isabella Scott, parents of William Johnston in Australia, 1855. [NRS.S/H]

JOHNSTON, Reverend JOHN, in Edinburgh, father of John R. Johnston in New Zealand, 1857. [NRS.S/H]

JOHNSTON, JOHN, MD, born in 1812, eldest son of Alexander Johnston, died in Asunction, Paraguay, on 9 October 1857. [St Cuthbert's gravestone, Edinburgh]

JOHNSTON, ROBERT, son of Henry Johnston in Meadowbank, died in Quebec on 2 April 1824. [EA]

JOHNSTON, Mrs, a silk and shawl cleaner, 21 Carnegie Street, Edinburgh, 1849. [POD]

JOLLIE, MARTIN, from Georgia, died in Antigua Street, Edinburgh, on 16 December 1806. [SM.69.78][TNA.AO.12/101/222, etc]

JONES, CONSTANCE, wife of A. M. Hetfield in Argyle, Shelbourne, Nova Scotia, daughter and heir of Anthony Hart Jones, there, in 1813. [NRS.S/H]

JONES, WILLIAM, a skipper in Leith, dead by 1798, brother of Anthony Hart Jones in Argyle, Nova Scotia. [NRS.S/H]

JONES, WILLIAM, born 1793 in Leith, a mariner, died in Savanna, Georgia, on 21 July 1809. [Savanna Death Register]

JORDAN, JANET, born 1799, died 1 October 1886. [South Leith church window]

JORDAN, JOHN, born 1830, a merchant in Leith, died 1914. [South Leith church window]

JUNOR, WILLIAM, born 1790, from Edinburgh, manager of the Colonial Bank in Jamaica, died on 9 May 1853. [St Andrew's gravestone, Jamaica]

KALLEY, ROBERT REID, MD, born on 8 September 1809, a teacher and a pastor in Rio de Janeiro and in Pernambuco, Brazil, from 1855 until his death on 17 January 1888. [Dean gravestone, Edinburgh]

KAY, ALEXANDER, born 1805, a plumber in Princes Street, Edinburgh, died on 28 February 1847, husband of Jemima Kidd, born 1811, died 13 September 1885. [St Cuthbert's gravestone]

KAY, DAVID, in Kinsman Township, Ohio, son and heir of Margaret Murray, wife of David Kay, a merchant in Leith, later in Glasgow, who died on 7 February 1854; also, heir to his uncle John Murray, a Captain in the Service of the East India Company, who died on 18 May 1832. [NRS.S/H]

KAY, WILLIAM, son of William Kay in Montreal, Quebec, heir to his grand-uncle Alexander Hutchison, a wine merchant in Edinburgh, in 1793. [NRS.S/H]

KEDDIE, ROBERT, son of John Keddie a candlemaker in Edinburgh, settled in New South Wales, Australia, by 1840. [NRS.S/H]

KEDSLIE, JOHN, [1846-1902], and his wife Margaret McNellan, parents of John A. Kedslie, born 1872, died in New Orleans, Louisiana, on 16 February 1891. [South Leith gravestone]

KEIR, ADAM, a brewer in Edinburgh, son of Margaret Gray or Keir, settled in New Zealand before 1848. [NRS.S/H]

KEITH, JAMES, son of William Keith an accountant in Edinburgh, was apprenticed to Bell, Wardrop, and Russell, surgeon apothecaries in Edinburgh for five years on 6 February 1800. [ERA]

KEITH, JAMES, an artists' colourman at 60 Princes Street, Edinburgh, in 1849. [POD]

KEITH, WILLIAM, of Corstorphin Hill, died on 25 October 1803. [Greyfriars gravestone]

KELLETT, RICHARD, MD, from Edinburgh, in the Service of the East India Company, died on 16 March 1835, an inventory 1835. [NRS]

KELLY, JOHN, a shipmaster in Leith, inventory, 1813, Comm. Edinburgh. [NRS]; testament, 1824. [NRS]

KEMP, JAMES, in Edinburgh, father of William Finnie Kemp who married Isobel Matson, youngest daughter of Charles Matson of Rio de Janeiro, Brazil, there on 10 May 1877. [S.10555]

KENNEDY, CHARLES, born 1787 in Edinburgh, a mariner who was naturalised in Charleston, South Carolina, on 24 January 1805. [NARA.M1183.1]

KENNEDY, DANIEL, a livestock agent in Edinburgh, father of Alexander Kennedy, a merchant in Chaneral, Chile, who married Jane Peebles, second daughter of Robert Peebles of Chaneral, in Valparaiso, Chile, on 22 November 1877. [S.10762]; also, father of Ewan Kennedy, who died in Chaneral, Chile, on 12 October 1879. [S.11.352]

KENNEDY, JAMES, son of Alexander Kennedy a cooper in Virginia, was apprenticed to Phin and Paterson, merchants in Edinburgh, for five years on 16 May 1798. [ERA]

KENNEDY, Mrs JOAN, born 1800 in Edinburgh, wife of Dr A. J. Kennedy, emigrated to America around 1818, died in Camden, South Carolina, in November 1823. [SC.26.11.1823]

KENNEY, Dr ANDREW, a physician from Edinburgh, died in Concordia, Tobago, on 13 January 1826. [S.651.216]

KENNOCH, A., an iron-founder, 59 Abbeyhill, Edinburgh, in 1849. [POD]

KERR, ANN BLAIR, born 1789 in Edinburgh, settled in Charleston, South Carolina, in 1789, was naturalised there on 31 October 1810. [NARA.M1183.1]

KERR, FRANCIS, second son of William Kerr the Surveyor General of the Post Office in Edinburgh, died in New York on 8 November 1805. [SM.68.78]

KERR, HELEN, eldest daughter of James Kerr in Quebec, married Thomas Duncan of Gouyave, Grenada, in Leith on 22 November 1827. [S.822.750]

KERR, JAMES, born 1764, son of Robert Kerr in Leith, educated at Glasgow University, admitted to the English Bar, emigrated to Canada in 1794, a judge and councillor from 1797 to 1827, Speaker of the Council 1826-1827, died in Quebec on 5 May 1846. [MAGU.151]

KERR, JAMES LEE, in St Thomas, Jamaica, brother and heir of Grace Kerr, wife of James Fitzgerald Grant in Edinburgh, also to his father Alexander Kerr, a merchant in Edinburgh, in 1853. [NRS.S/H]

KERR, JOHN CAMPBELL, a saddler from Edinburgh, emigrated via Greenock to Canada in 1815. [TNA.CO385.2]; brother and heir of George Kerr, a writer in Edinburgh, in 1839. [NRS.S/H]

KERR, JOHN, at Three Rivers, Canada, nephew and heir to Mary Learmont in Edinburgh, in 1855. [NRS.S/H]

KERR, JOHN, late of Corunna Place, Bonnington Road, Leith, died in St Luis, South America, on 2 January 1873. [S.9202]

KERR, JOHN, born 1821, died in Melbourne, Victoria, Australia, on 6 February 1874. [St Cuthbert's gravestone]

KERR, MAGDALENE, in St Bernard's Crescent, Edinburgh, died on 19 June 1841, relict of George Meikle, a surgeon in the Service of the East India Company, an inventory 1841. [NRS]

KERR, WILLIAM, and Son, merchants in Leith, sederunt book, 1822. [NRS.CS96.847]; trading with St Petersburg, Russia, and Riga, Latvia, in 1822. [NRS.CS233.SEQN.K1/12]

KERR, WILLIAM, born 1840, from 80 South Clerk Street, Edinburgh, died at Minas Schweger, Coronel, Chile, on 18 October 1883. [S.12610]

KERR, ..., born in Leith, son of a merchant, educated at Leith Grammar School and Glasgow University, emigrated to Canada in 1794, a politician and lawyer, died in Quebec on 5 May 1846. [DCB]

KID, DAVID, a merchant and fish-curer in Leith, a journal from 1815 until 1819. [NRS.CS96.3984]

KIDD, or TODDIE, JANET, in Edinburgh, heir to Lindsay Toddie, a cotton planter in America, in 1833. [NRS.S/H]

KILGOUR, J., a tea and coffee dealer, 75 Tolbooth Wynd, Leith, 1849. [POD]

KILGOUR, MARY, born 29 May 1773, daughter of David Kilgour and his wife Agnes Scotland, died in Portobello, Midlothian, on 8 October 1854. [St Cuthbert's gravestone, Edinburgh]

KILGOUR, WILLIAM, a merchant in Edinburgh, father of Peter Martin Kilgour in Calcutta, India, 1855. [NRS.S/H]

KINCAID, MARGARET, daughter of Thomas Kincaid a merchant in Leith, married Alexander Rowand MD from Montreal, Quebec, in Edinburgh on 25 December 1843. [W.5.430][GM.NS21.309]

KINGHORN, HUGH, born 1769, a builder in Leith, died 23 July 1838, husband of [1] Alison Henderson, born 1779, died 11 November 1811, [2] Susan Addie, born 1781, died 25 January 1848. [South Leith gravestone]

KINGHORN, WILLIAM, born 1801, of Bonnington Villa, Leith, died 16 April 1874, husband of Catherine Murphy, born 1803, died 29 January 1860. [South Leith gravestone]

KINNEAR, ALEXANDER, a banker in Edinburgh, died at Heriot Hill, Edinburgh, on 26 November 1819. [SM.85]

KINNEAR, DAVID, born 1807 in Edinburgh, Proprietor of the 'Montreal Herald', died in Montreal on 20 November 1862. [GM.ns2/14.127]

KINNEL, Mrs, a nurse, 5 St James' Place, Edinburgh, 1849. [POD]

KIPPEN, JAMES, in Salt Lake City, Utah, brother and heir of Duncan Kippen, a spirit dealer in Edinburgh, who died on 24 April 1879. [NRS.S/H]

KIRBY, THOMAS JEREMIAH SMITH, only son of Jeremiah Kirby MD, died in Edinburgh on 19 September 1822. [SM.90.632]

KIRKLAND, J., merchant, 21 Baltic Street, Edinburgh, 1849. [POD]

KIRKWOOD, ALEXANDER, born 1818 in Edinburgh, died aboard the William Nicol of Glasgow on 7 April 1839. [Scotch Burial Ground, Calcutta, India]

KNIGHT, WILLIAM, a slater from Edinburgh, died in the East Indies on 15 March 1824, an inventory 1830. [NRS]

KNOX, JAMES, son of James Knox and his wife Mary........, was born on 15 December 1797 and baptised in the church of St John the Evangelist in Edinburgh on 17 December 1797. [NRS.CH12.3.26.2]

KNOX, JAMES, a surveyor in Tipperlinn, Edinburgh, 1849. [POD]

KNOX, JOHN, son of James Knox in Charles Street, Edinburgh, a partner in the firm Knox and Lawrie merchants in New York, died near New York on 18 July 1810. [EA.4870.1411] [ANY]

KNOX, WILLIAM, son of James Knox and his wife Mary........, was born on 2 November 1799 and baptised in the church of St John the Evangelist in Edinburgh on 2 November 1799. [NRS.CH12.3.26.7]

LAIDLAW, BARBARA, third daughter of ..... Laidlaw of Johnston Place, Stockbridge, Edinburgh, married James Cross from St John, Newfoundland, in Edinburgh n 6 March 1820. [BM.7.118]

LAIDLAW, R., Venetian blind maker, Simon Square, Edinburgh, 1849. [POD]

LAING, AGNES, wife of Thomas Rule in Lisbon, New York, heir to Cecilia Laing, widow of John Lauder, a victual dealer in Canongait, Edinburgh, who died on 30 September 1863. [NRS.S/H]

LAING, GEORGE, a writer in Edinburgh, was admitted as a burgess and guildsbrother of Dunfermline on 16 June 1796. [DM]

LAING, JOHN, a japanner, 8 Calton Hill, Edinburgh, in 1849. [POD]

LAIRD, A., a salt warehouseman, 22 Constitution Street, Edinburgh, 1849. [POD]

LAMB, JOHN, a skipper in Leith, testament, 20 January 1792, Comm. Edinburgh. [NRS]

L'AMY, JAMES, of Dunkenny, the younger, married Mary Carson, second daughter of Dr John Carson, a physician in Philadelphia,

Pennsylvania, widow of William Carson O'Hare in Pittsburgh, Pennsylvania, in Edinburgh on 5 November 1811. [SM.73.877]

LANCEFIELD, A., a surveyor, 11 Buccleuch Place, Edinburgh, 1849. [POD]

LANCEFIELD, WILLIAM ADAMS, from Edinburgh later in America, brother and heir of Alfred Henry Lancefield, son of Alfred Lancefield, a civil engineer in London, in 1870. [NRS.S/H]

LANG, JOHN WILLIAM, born 1835, son of William Lang and his wife Isabella Murray, a surgeon in Mexico, died in Southampton, England, on 18 February 1865. [St Cuthbert's gravestone]

LAPSLEY, J., a perfumer, 14 Hanover Street, Edinburgh, 1849. [POD]

LAUDER, GEORGE, born 24 January 1810 in Edinburgh, a post-master and marble cutter, died in North Carolina on 31 May 1888. [Cross Creek gravestone, N.C.]

LAUDER, JAMES, a historical painter, 24 Fettes Row, Edinburgh, 1849. [POD]

LAW, ALEXANDER, elder of South Leith parish in 1825. [SLR]; a distiller in Leith, a petitioner in 1828; an elder on 1 October 1843. [SLR]

LAURIE, JAMES, born 1832, a blacksmith from Edinburgh, emigrated aboard the Donald McKay bound for Australia, landed in Hobart, Tasmania, Australia, on 6 September 1855. [SRA.TD292]

LAWRIE, ROBERT, born 1803, a merchant in Leith, died on 4 February 1874; husband of Mary Scott, born 1797, died 17 January 1871. [St Cuthbert's gravestone, Edinburgh]

LAWRIE, THOMAS, a sailor in Leith, inventory, 1813, Comm. Edinburgh. [NRS.SC70.1.7.658]

LEARMONTH, ALEXANDER, from Edinburgh, a tanner and merchant in Charleston, South Carolina, died before 1800. [NRS.NRAS.0063]

LEARMONT, JAMES, born 1785, an iron-founder in Edinburgh, died on 13 May 1842, his wife Elizabeth Mitchell, born 1814, died on 4 February 1854. [St Cuthbert's gravestone, Edinburgh]

LEARMONTH, T., a bell-hanger of 10 Barony Street, Edinburgh, in 1849. [POD]

LEASK, J. B., an ironmonger, 10 Tolbooth Wynd, Leith, in 1849. [POD]

LECKIE, GEORGE, from Edinburgh, settled in New York before 1841. [ANY]

LECKIE, JOHN, was educated at Edinburgh University, a teacher at New York University Grammar School, died on 22 August 1841. [ANY]

LEDINGHAM, ALEXANDER, a merchant from Leith, died at Crane Wharf, Black River, Jamaica, on 19 January 1823. [SM][S.338.224]

LEGGAT, ANDREW, born 1805, son of Andrew Leggat, [1780-1827], a whip manufacturer, and his wife Helen Hume, [1774-1837], died in New York on 1 June 1827. [Greyfriars gravestone, Edinburgh] [S.794.528]

LEGGAT, DAVID, born 1810, son of Alexander Leggat and his wife Wilhelmina Hutchison, died in New York on 16 December 1842. [St Cuthbert's gravestone, Edinburgh]

LEGGAT, GIDEON, born 1791, son of James Leggat, [1764-1845], and his wife Mary Wilson, [1768-1818], died in Virginia in 1838. [New Calton gravestone, Edinburgh]

LEGGAT, G., a whip and thong maker, 4 Brown Square, Edinburgh, 1849. [POD]

LEIGHTON, ELIZABETH, wife of George Bowman, a baker in New York, daughter and heir of Francis Leighton in Edinburgh, who died on 10 November 1843. [NRS.S/H]

LEIGHTON, THOMAS, in East Cambridge, Boston, Massachusetts, letters, 1838-1848. [NRAS.206]

LEITH, MARY ELIZABETH ANNE, daughter of Colonel James Leith and his wife Augusta ……., was born on 17 November 1798 and baptised in the church of St John the Evangelist in Edinburgh on 21 December 1798. [NRS.CH12.3.26.5]

LENDRUM, R., bookseller, 25 Hanover Street, Edinburgh, 1849. [POD]

LENNIE, J., a jeweller, gold and silversmith, 14 Leith Street, Edinburgh, in 1849. [POD]

LESLIE, GEORGE, born 1743 in Edinburgh, a merchant who died at Cape Vincent, America, on 7 May 1823. [EA]

LESLIE, JOHN ALEXANDER, an accountant with the Bank of British North America in Toronto, Ontario, sister and heir of Arabella Leslie in Edinburgh, who died on 18 December 1868. [NRS.S/H]

LESLIE, THOMAS, of the brig Princess of Wales of Leith, died in Jamaica on 6 February 1797. [CM.11803]

LEVEN, JAMES, born 1829, son of John Leven an Excise collector, died in Maccio, Brazil, on 9 March 1850. [Canongait gravestone]

LEVIE, MARGARET, in Sherriff Brae, South Leith, was granted a beggar's badge on 18 February 1794. [SLR]

LEVY, M.A., woollen draper, South Bridge, Edinburgh, 1849. [POD]

LEWIS, ..., a medical student from Barbados, died in Nicolson Street, Edinburgh, on 22 January 1804. [SM.66.80]

LEWIS, Miss, teacher of elocution,22 Rutland Square, Edinburgh, 1849. [POD]

LIDDLE, ELSPETH, in South Gray's Close, Edinburgh, daughter and heir of Mrs Janet Liddle, wife of Thomas Liddle in New York, in 1860. [NRS.S/H]

LIDDELL, EVAN, deacon of South Leith parish in 1825. [SLR]; a merchant in Leith, a petitioner in 1828. [SLR]

LIDDELL, THOMAS, in 161 West Fountainbridge, Edinburgh, father of Alexander Liddell, born 1858, died in Havanna, Cuba, on 17 August 1878. [S.10967]

LIGHTBODY, JOHAN BUCHAN, youngest daughter of Mrs Lightbody in Buccleuch Place, Edinburgh, married George Thistle Geden, a merchant from St John's, Newfoundland, in Glasgow on 26 September 1822. [DPCA.10541]

LINDSAY, GEORGE, a surgeon in New York, heir to his grandfather James Stalker, a teacher in Edinburgh, also, heir to his mother Margaret Stalker or Lindsay in Edinburgh, in 1841. [NRS.S/H]

LINDSAY, Captain JAMES, born 1786 in Leith, a shipowner, died 26 March 1839, husband of Helen Allan, born 1786 in Alloa, died 10 April 1849. [South Leith gravestone]

LINDSAY, JOHN, a surgeon, an author, and a Fellow of the Royal Society of Edinburgh, died in Savanna-la-Mar, Jamaica, in September 1803. [SM.65.885]

LINDSAY, WALLACE, Fellow of the Royal College of Physicians of Edinburgh, born 30 May 1837, son of James Lindsay, [1804-1874], and his wife Helen Baird Lauder, [1804-1883], an assistant surgeon of the 30th Regiment, died in Cordsal, British Honduras, on 31 December 1862. [Dean gravestone] [S.2405]

LINDSAY, WILLIAM, elder of South Leith parish in 1825. [SLR]; a merchant in Leith, a petitioner in 1828. [SLR]

LINDSAY, WILLIAM, born 1843, youngest son of Robert Lindsay in Edinburgh, a typefounder in Chicago, Illinois, died in Brooklyn, New York, on 27 April 1885. [S.13057]

LINN, GEORGE, a machinist in Belleville, Ontario, heir to Margaret Waldie, wife of Henry Linn in Edinburgh, who died on 1 December 1868. [NRS.S/H]

LITHGOW, ROBERT, born 1758, son of …. Lithgow in Leith, died on his estate on Colonel's Island, Georgia, on 11 October 1802. [EA.4077.03]

LITTLEJOHN, T., a confectioner in 31 Leith Street, Edinburgh, 1849. [POD]

LIVINGSTONE, J., a grocer and spirit dealer, 30 Water Lane, Leith, 1849. [POD]

LIZARS, WILLIAM, son of William Leith a shoemaker in Leith, in Georgetown, British Guiana, in 1833. [NRS.S/H]

LIZARS, W. H., a copperplate printer, 3 St James Square, Edinburgh, 1849. [POD]

LOCKE, Mrs CATHERINE, wife of James Bruce, the naval officer in Leith, died in St John, New Brunswick, on 4 February 1834. [FJ.66][AJ.4501]

LOCKHART, ROBERT, son of Robert Lockhart late of the East India Company, was apprenticed to William and John Crawford, merchants in Leith, for five years on 29 November 1799. [ERA]

LOGAN, HUGH, a ship carver, 49 Timber Bush, Leith, 1849. [POD]

LONGMORE, ELIZA FRANCES, daughter of George Longmore of the Medical Staff in Quebec, died in Edinburgh on 21 October 1823. [S.380.360]

LORIMER, GEORGE, and his wife Margaret Wilkie, parents of Henry James Lorimer, born 1854, died in San Jose, California, on 17 September 1891. [St Cuthbert's gravestone, Edinburgh]

LORIMER, JOHN, MD, born 21 August 1837, son of John Lorimer, a builder, and his wife Christian Mathieson, died in Batavia, Java, Dutch East Indies, on 8 January 1872. [St Cuthbert's gravestone]

LOTHIAN, PATRICK, a mariner in New York, died 23 May 1793, brother of Walter Lothian a merchant in Edinburgh, testament, 1824. [NRS.CC8.8.150]

LOW, JOHN PARK, in New York, son and heir of John Low, a china merchant in Edinburgh, in 1854. [NRS.S/H]

LOWRIE, WILLIAM, a paper ruler, 13 Blair Street, Edinburgh, 1849. [POD]

LUMSDEN, JAMES, in Leith in 1800. [NRS.CS234.seqn.s9.1/22]

LUTHMAN, CHARLES, in Edinburgh, applied to settle in Canada on 28 February 1815. [NRS.RH9]

LYSCHINSKI, A., a medical practitioner, 10 Warriston Crescent, Edinburgh, 1849. [POD]

LYONS, BURRISH, a shipmaster in Leith, testament, 1807, Comm. Edinburgh. [NRS.CC8.8.137.131]

LYON, JOHN, an elder of South Leith parish on 1 October 1843. [SLR]

LYON, RICHARD, a picture frame maker, in St Andrew Lane, Edinburgh, 1849. [POD]

MCALPINE, WILLIAM, son of James McAlpine a butcher in Leith, was apprenticed to Archibald Ronaldson, a butcher in Edinburgh, for five years on 12 January 1797. [ERA]

MACARTNEY, JAMES, a merchant in Mexico, died in Edinburgh on 22 August 1839, testament, 1839, Edinburgh. [NRS.SC70.1.58/426]

MCAULAY, GEORGE KELLIE, chief engineer of HMS Brisk, second son of Dr Alexander McAulay in Edinburgh, died on Vancouver Island, Canada, on 1 August 1855. [SG.2.152]

MCBEAN, JAMES, Lieutenant Colonel of the 78th Highlanders, died on 23 October 1845, his wife Elizabeth Robertson, died on 7 November 1832, parents of John McBean an assistant surgeon of the 50th Regiment, who died in Lucca, Jamaica, on 17 January 1850, also of George McBean, who died in Brighton, Australia, on 23 November 1860. [St Cuthbert's gravestone]

MACCALL, EDWARD, a teacher in Edinburgh, versus his wife Elizabeth Hislop, a Process of Divorce in 1809. [NRS.CC8.5.31]

MCCALL, Captain, master of the Buchehelus of Leith from Leith to Melbourne, Victoria, Australia, in January 1857, landed there on 7 June 1857. [LCL.4583/4646]

MCCLUMPHA, JOHN, tailor, Queensferry Street, Edinburgh, 1849. [POD]

MCCOLL, THOMAS, master of the St Laurence of Leith from Greenock bound for Newfoundland in 1818. [NRS.E504.15.120]

MCCRAE, JOHN MORISON, born 8 May 1804 in Edinburgh, son of William Gordon McCrae and his wife Margaret Morison, an Ensign of the 17th Bengal Native Infantry, died in Ludhiana, Punjab, India, on 15 June 1822. [BA]

MCCRAE, MARY HARVIE, eldest daughter of William Gordon McCrae, married Francis Cobham, MD, from Barbados, in Edinburgh on 2 August 1820. [BM.7.705]

MCCRIE, WILLIAM, a paper hanging manufacturer, 22 Leith Walk, Edinburgh, 1849. [POD]

MCCULLOCH, Mrs JESSIE, of 90 Abbey Hill, Edinburgh, relict of Reverend Alexander Webster in the Service of the East India Company in Madras, India, died on 4 August 1840, inventory 1840. [NRS]

MCCULLOCH, WILLIAM, born 28 February 1816 in the parish of St Cuthbert's, Edinburgh, son of John Ramsay McCulloch and his wife Isabella Stewart, a Lieutenant Colonel of the 13th Bengal Native Infantry, died in Shillong, Assam, India, on 4 April 1885. [BA]

MCDIARMID, FINLAY, in Aldborough, Canada, cousin and heir of John McDiarmid in Edinburgh, a Captain of the Rifle Brigade, in 1847. [NRS.S/H]

MCDONAGH, WILLIAM, a confectioner in 14 Kirkgate, Edinburgh, 1849. [OD]

MCDONALD, ANGUS, innkeeper, Ship Inn, Newhaven, Edinburgh, in 1849. [POD]

MACDONALD, JAMES, a blacksmith in Edinburgh with his wife and four children, emigrated via Edinburgh to Canada in 1815. [TNA.CO385.2]

MCDONALD, JAMES, in Edinburgh, son and heir of Daniel McDonald, a smith from Edinburgh later in America, in 1835. [NRS.S/H]

MACDONALD, JOHN, born 17 February 1807 in Edinburgh, landed in Calcutta, India, on 4 February 1838, a missionary in India from 1838 until his death on 1 September 1847. [F.7.698] [Scotch Burial Ground gravestone, Calcutta]

MCDONALD, JOHN, a labourer and pensioner in Edinburgh, emigrated via Greenock to Canada in 1815. [TNA.CO385.2]

MCDONALD, JOHN, a surgeon from Edinburgh, with Margaret his wife, emigrated via Greenock to Canada in 1815. [TNA.CO385.2]

MACDONALD, RANALD, in Girnish, Canada, nephew and heir of Allan MacDonald from Edinburgh, later on Prince Edward Island, in 1853. [NRS.S/H]

MACDONALD, RODRICK, born 1804, a Lieutenant of the Bengal Army, died in Edinburgh on 3 March 1837. [St Cuthbert's gravestone, Edinburgh]

MCEWAN, JOHN, Sergeant Major of H Company of the 65th Regiment of Illinois Volunteer Infantry, died in the US Civil War, 1861-1865. [Old Calton gravestone, Edinburgh]

MCEWAN, WILLIAM, a physician in Jamaica, brother and heir of John McEwan, a writer in Edinburgh, in 1785. [NRS.S/H]

MCFARLANE, HUGH, born 1840, died in New York on 15 April 1876. [St Cuthbert's gravestone, Edinburgh]

MCFARLANE, ISABELLA, eldest daughter of Mr McFarlane on Long Island, America, died in Minto Street, Newington, Edinburgh, on 26 January 1829. [S.946.72]

MCFARLANE, JOHN, son of Duncan McFarlane an innkeeper in Leith, was apprenticed to William McEwan, a gunsmith in Edinburgh, for seven years, on 13 November 1794. [ERA]

MCFARLANE, JOHN, born 1781 in Edinburgh, a plasterer, died in South Carolina on 24 January 1805. [Old Scots gravestone, Charleston, S.C.]

MCFARLANE, PETER, late Rector of Leith High School, died in Monte Video, Uruguay, on 8 September 1870. [S8512]; testament, 1871. [NRS.SC70.1.151/94]

MCFARQUHAR, JOHN, a police watchman in Edinburgh, accused of theft in 1815. [NRS.AD14.15.13]

MCGIBBON, CHARLES, born 1843, died in New York on 10 January 1872. [New Calton gravestone, Edinburgh]

MCGIBBON, CHRISTINA, born 1800, wife of Reverend William Rintoul in Montreal, Quebec, died on 7 August 1855. [New Calton gravestone, Edinburgh]

MACGIBBON, DAVID MOYES, MD, [1796-1835], surgeon of the 35th Regiment, husband of Elizabeth Wickham, died 1834, parents of Christina MacGibbon, wife of Reverend William Rintoul in Montreal, Quebec, who died on 7 August 1885. [New Calton gravestone]

MCGLASHAN, JOHN, in Feliz Valley, California, son and heir of William McGlashan, a vintner in Edinburgh, who died on 26 May 1831. [NRS.S/H]

MACGLASHAN, JOHN, from Kingston, Jamaica, married Eliza Jane Turner, eldest daughter of Dutton Smith Turner of Clarendon, Jamaica, in Edinburgh on 17 January 1827. [BM.21.373]

MCGLASHAN, JOHN, in Georgia, son and heir of James McGlashan, a grocer in Edinburgh, who died on 23 April 1849. [NRS.S/H]

MCGLASHAN, NEIL, born 1809, died in New York on 5 January 1864. [South Leith gravestone]

MCGREGOR, or CAMPBELL, CATHERINE, born 1797, eldest daughter of Alexander McGregor in St Andrew's Square, Edinburgh, married Ewan McPherson from Demerara, in Edinburgh in 1817. [S.17.17]; and as widow of Evan McPherson, died in Georgetown, Demerara, on 23 March 1822. [BM.11.768]

MCGREGOR, DONALD, a painter in Philadelphia, Pennsylvania, brother and heir of Margaret McGregor in Edinburgh, and to his brother David MacGregor, a bookseller in Edinburgh, in 1857. [NRS.S/H]

MACGREGOR, JAMES, a merchant, only son of Alexander McGregor, of St Andrew's Square, Edinburgh, died in Georgetown, Demerara, on 12 June 1825. [BM.18.655]

MCGREGOR, JAMES, from Edinburgh, father of John Anderson McGregor, born 1868, died in Santiago, Chile, on 25 July 1870. [S.8478]

MCGREGOR, JOHN B., in Leith, applied to settle in Canada on 28 February 1815. [NRS.RH9]

MCGREGOR, JOSEPH ROBERTSON, minister of the Gaelic congregation, only son of Captain MacGregor of the 88th Regiment, died on 12 January 1801. [Greyfriars gravestone]

MCGRUGAR, THOMAS, a merchant, died on 10 May 1799, husband of Agnes Hogg, died 7 January 1802. [Greyfriars gravestone]

MACHARG, MARIA, born 1812, daughter of Captain James MacHarg of the Bengal Military Service, in India, died on 1 January 1831. [Duddingston gravestone]

MCHENRY, Mrs MARION, born 1795 in Edinburgh, married James McHenry in Savanna, Georgia, died in Lexington, Oglethorpe County, Ga., on 22 October 1822. [Georgia Journal, 5.11.1822]

MACINTOSH, JOHN, born 1734, 'an accountant with the Bank of Scotland for nearly 40 years', died on 21 July 1820. [Greyfriars gravestone]

MACINTYRE, DUNCAN BAN, born on 20 March 1724 in Glen Orchy, 'the celebrated Celtic bard', died in Edinburgh on 14 May 1812. [Greyfriars gravestone]

MACIVER, JANET, in Warden's Land, South Leith, was granted a beggar's badge on 18 February 1794. [SLR]

MCKAY, ALEXANDER, from Leith, later in Altoda, Tahuel, Chile, married Jeannie Brunton, eldest daughter of George Brunton of Valparaiso, Chile, there on 11 December 1872. [S.8918]

MACKAY, DANIEL, from St Croix, Danish Virgin Islands, married Mrs Muir, widow of John Muir of Demerara, in Morningside, Edinburgh, on 17 February 1825. [BM.17.638] [GM.95/273]

MCKEAN, WILLIAM BLAIR, [1799-1875], and his wife Marianne McCulloch, parents of Alexander Charles McKean who died in San Francisco, California, in August 1869. [Greyfriars gravestone, Edinburgh]

MCKECHNIE, JOHN, a medical student in Edinburgh, later a physician in Demerara by 1809. [NRS.CS17.1.20/511]

MACKENZIE, ALEXANDER, a coach-painter in USA, nephew and heir

of Hannah McDonald, widow of James Dick, a cabinetmaker in Edinburgh, in 1859. [NRS.S/H]

MCKENZIE, Miss JANE, from Demerara, died in Edinburgh on 3 September 1825, testament, 1836, Edinburgh. [NRS]

MACKENZIE, JOHN, born 1746, late from Jamaica, died in Catharine Street, Edinburgh, on 18 September 1813. [SM]

MCKENZIE, JOHN, third son of Charles McKenzie a writer in Edinburgh, died in Demerara in 1802. [GkAd.54]

MACKENZIE, JOHN, born 1755, eldest son of William MacKenzie of Belmaduthie in Ross-shire, a Lieutenant General who died in 1833. [St John's gravestone, Edinburgh]

MACKENZIE, J., a silver plater, 11 Carruber's Close, Edinburgh, 1849. [POD]

MACKENZIE, MARY, wife of Thomas Campsie, a carpenter in New York, nephew and heir of Hannah McDonald, widow of James Dick, a cabinetmaker in Edinburgh, in 1859. [NRS.S/H]

MACKIE, JAMES, a shipmaster in Leith, testament, 1808, Comm. Edinburgh. [NRS.CC8.8.137.171]

MACKIE, WILLIAM, a jeweller from Edinburgh later in Cuba, son and heir of Charles Mackie, a jeweller in London, in 1826. [NRS.S/H]

MCKENZIE, WILLIAM, from Edinburgh, was naturalised in Charleston, South Carolina, on 5 October 1831. [NARA.M1183.1]

MACKIE, ..., master of the Agnes of Leith, from Leith to Quebec in 1823. [EEC.17433]

MACLACHLAN, ALEXANDER, a writer in Edinburgh, testament, 1793, Comm. Edinburgh. [NRS]

MCLACHLAN, JOHN CLARK, of the Edinburgh Militia, nephew and heir to Allan McLachlan in Tobago, in 1814. [NRS.S/H]

MACLAGAN, Dr DAVID PHILIP, assistant surgeon aboard HMS Icarus, eldest son of Dr Douglas MaccLagan in Edinburgh, died in the Ruatan Bay Islands, Honduras, on 27 June 1860. [S.1591] [DC.23522]

MCLAREN, AGNES, MD, born 4 July 1837, daughter of Duncan McLaren, died on 18 April 1913, buries in Antibes, France. [St Cuthbert's gravestone]

MACLAREN, DAVID, a merchant in Leith, testaments, 1789, 1793, Comm. Edinburgh. [NRS]

MACLAREN, GEORGE ADINSTON, born 1801, a wine merchant in Leith and Provost from 1848 to 1851, Chairman of the Parochial Board from 1852 to 1880, died in 1881. [South Leith church window]

MCLAREN, DAVID and WILLIAM, corn merchants in Constitution Street, Leith, a bond of caution for Michael Mitzlaff in Elbing, Prussia, in 1850s. [NRS.SC11.62.4.28]

MCLAREN, ISABELLA, born 1826 in Newhaven, North Leith, daughter of Alexander McLaren a fisherman, was accused of theft at Auchenleck's Brae, Newhaven, in 1849. [NRS.AD14.49.9]

MCLAREN, JOHN, a surgeon from Edinburgh, died in Kingston, Jamaica, on 12 January 1822. [BM.11.502]

MCLAREN, WILLIAM, a shipmaster in Leith, testament, 1828, Comm. Edinburgh. [NRS]

MCLAUGHLAN, ANDREW, in New York, son and heir of George McLaughlan in Edinburgh, who died in 1836. [NRS.S/H]

MCLAURIN, Mrs, widow of Ewan McLaurin in Charleston, America, and sister of Bain Whyte, a Writer to the Signet in Edinburgh, died in Demerara on 29 December 1822. [SM.91.519]

MCLEAN, ANDREW, a basket maker at 61 Tolbooth Wynd, Leith, in 1849. [POD]

MCLEAN, HECTOR, third son of D. McLean, a Writer to the Signet in Edinburgh, died in Spanish Town, Jamaica, on 26 June 1818. [S.96.18]

MCLEISH, ISABELLA, wife of T. E. Sharpe in Boston, Massachusetts, son and heir of David McLeish, a cooper in Edinburgh, who died in February 1849. [NRS.S/H]

MCLENNAN, Mrs, a nurse, 39 India Place, Edinburgh, 1849. [POD]

MCLEOD, ISABEL, in Workman's Land, South Leith, was granted a beggar's badge on 18 February 1794. [SLR]

MCLEOD, THOMAS, in New Baltimore, America, son and heir of George McLeod, a printer in Edinburgh, who died on 7 June 1852. [NRS.S/H]

MCLUCKIE, JAMES, master James MacLuckie, from Inverkeithing to Quebec in 1812. [NRS.E504.16.1]; a shipmaster in Leith, died in Calcutta, India, on 18 July 1827, testament, 1828, Comm. Edinburgh. [NRS.CC8.8.152.34]

MCMILLAN, JOHN, second son of John McMillan of Edinburgh High School, married Elizabeth Barry Craswell, eldest daughter of William Craswell, in Monte Video, Uruguay, on 15 July 1863. [S.2561]

MCMILLAN, MICHAEL, a carter in Edinburgh, was accused of theft in 1820. [NRS.AD14.20.98]

MCNAUGHT, J., a confectioner of 45 North Bridge, Edinburgh, 1849. [POD]

MCNEILL, GEORGE, son of Archibald McNeill and his wife Georgina Anne …., was born on 6 July 1798 and baptised in the church of St John the Evangelist on 20 July 1798. [NRS.CH12.3.26.5]

MCNICOL, JOHN, a skipper in Jamaica, inventory, 1814, Comm. Edinburgh. [NRS]

MCPHERSON, C., a tool manufacturer, 1 Gilmore Street, St Paul's Work, Edinburgh, 1849. [POD]

MCPHERSON, GILLIES, a carter in Edinburgh, was accused of theft in 1820. [NRS.AD14.20.98]

MCPHERSON, JOHN, born 1784 in Edinburgh, a merchant who drowned off Cape North, Labrador, on 9 September 1824. [S.529.80]

MCQUEEN, ALEXANDER, a coach hirer, 35 Northumberland Street, Edinburgh, 1849. [POD]

MCQUEEN, GEORGE, collector of the cess, died on 2 June 1795, husband of Janet Stirling who died on 26 July 1806. [Greyfriars gravestone]

MCQUILLEN, W., a dyer and scourer, 4 Portland Place, Edinburgh, 1849. [POD]

MACRAE, ALEXANDER, from Edinburgh via London to Norfolk, Virginia, in 1804-1805, five letters. [NRS.GD23]

MCRITCHIE, THOMAS, deacon of South Leith parish in 1825. [SLR]; a merchant in Leith, a petitioner in 1828; an elder on 1 October 1843. [SLR]

MCRONALD, ALEXANDER, a carpenter in Toronto, Ontario, son and heir of Thomas McRonald, a clerk of works in Edinburgh, who died on 27 April 1870. [NRS.S/H]

MACVICAR, DAVID, son of Neil McVicar of Fergushill, a writer in Edinburgh, and Master of Chancery, died in Spanish Town, Jamaica, on 13 January 1825. [BM.17.639]

MACVICAR, MARJORY, daughter of Neil McVicar of Fergushill, a writer in Edinburgh, and Master of Chancery, died in Kingston, Jamaica, on 23 October 1827. [BM.23.664]

MCWHIRTER, Dr J., in Edinburgh, father of John Peach McWhirter, who settled in Bengal, India, before 1849. [NRS.S/H]

MACK, Reverend JOHN, born on 12 March 1797 in Edinburgh, died in Serampore, Bengal, India, on 30 April 1845. [Serampore gravestone]

MAGAN, MARY ANNE, daughter of Michael Magan and Hannah .... his wife, was born on 3 September 1798 and baptised in the church of St John the Evangelist in Edinburgh on 26 November 1798. [NRS.CH12.3.26.5]

MAILER, ANDREW, a shoemaker, in Depere, Wisconsin, son and heir of Andrew Mailer, a mason in Edinburgh, who died on 31 December 1830. [NRS.S/H]

MAIR, Dr WILLIAM, from Edinburgh, died in Buenos Ayres, Argentina, on 10 July 1869. [S.8141]

MAITLAND, CHARLOTTE, daughter of Lieutenant Colonel Frederick Maitland and his wife Catherine Warsam, was born on 30 April 1799 and baptised in the church of St John the Evangelist in Edinburgh on 12 June 1799. [NRS.CH12.3.26.7]

MALCOLM, THOMAS, born 1845, eldest son of Thomas and Mary Malcolm from Edinburgh, died in New York on 20 March 1870. [S.8332]

MANSON, GEORGE WRIGHT, born on 16 June 1845 in Edinburgh, son of George Manson and his wife Janet Steele Reid, graduated from Edinburgh University in 1869, an Indian chaplain from 1870 until 1893, died in Edinburgh on 9 October 1915. [F.7.577]

MAR, JAMES, born in Edinburgh, settled in Boston, New England, died in New York on 19 November 1841. [EEC.20297]

MARJORYBANKS, J., master of the Lady Forbes of Leith, from Leith bound for New York and Jamaica in 1817. [NRS.E504.22.78]

MARK, SARA F., wife of P. Anderson, in Halifax, Nova Scotia, heir to her brother Alexander Mark, a writer in Edinburgh, who died on 4 April 1823. [NRS.S/H]

MARSHALL, or VALK, ANNE, in Carolina, heir to her brother James Marshall, a painter in Edinburgh, in 1831. [NRS.S/H]

MARSHALL, EUPHEMIA, born 27 April 1846, daughter of William Marshall an engineer and shipbuilder, died 6 April 1888. [South Leith church window]

MARSHALL, or CROWLEY, HANNAH, in Carolina, sister and heir of James Marshall, a painter in Edinburgh, in 1831. [NRS.S/H]

MARSHALL, JOHN, in Edinburgh, heir to his brother Joseph Marshall, a merchant in Jamaica, in 1836. [NRS.S/H]

MARSHALL, MARY C., in Philadelphia, Pennsylvania, heir to her grandfather Francis Marshall, a merchant in Edinburgh, in 1806. [NRS.S/H]

MARTIN, CATHERINE, in St John, New Brunswick, heir to her father James Martin, a stationer in Edinburgh, who died on 14 March 1868. [NRS.S/H]

MARTIN, or JOHNSTONE, ELIZABETH, in Chiccanoggo, USA, sister and heir of George Martin, a mason in Edinburgh, in 1833. [NRS.S/H]

MARTIN, ELIZABETH, daughter of Alexander Martin a land surveyor in Brooklyn, New York, married William Bennet a book-keeper from Edinburgh, in New York on 4 June 1853, died in Brooklyn on 8 May 1842. [FH]

MARTIN, JOHN, in Canada, cousin and heir of John Gillies, a surgeon in Edinburgh, who died on 24 November 1834. [NRS.S/H]

MARTIN, WILLIAM, a merchant in New York, died in Edinburgh on 4 May 1844. [ANY]

MARTIN, WILLIAM ALEXANDER, born 1818, son of William Alexander Martin, [1781-1828], a writer to the signet, and his wife Margaret Davie, [1788-1825], died in Tobago on 26 January 1850. [Greyfriars gravestone, Edinburgh]; in Tobago, heir to his great grandfather William Alexander, a wright in Edinburgh, in 1838; also, heir to his brother Peter Martin, in the Service of the East India Company, in 1849. [NRS.S/H]

MASON, JAMES, master of the Skeen of Leith from Leith bound for New York in 1816, from Leith bound for Halifax, Nova Scotia, in 1817 and 1818. [NRS.E504.22.73, 76, 80]

MASON, JANE SUSANNAH, daughter of Mr Mason formerly of the Theatre Royal in Edinburgh, niece of the late John Kemble and Mrs Sidons, married Henry Hillyard artist of the Park Theatre, in New York on 23 November 1839, [S.24.2090]

MASON, JOHN, from Leith, died in Santos, Brazil, on 1 September 1863. [S.2592]

MASON, WILLIAM, born 1 October 1801, a Solicitor of the Supreme Court, died 27 May 1874, husband of Rachel Stuart Sanderson, born 7 April 1822, died on 5 February 1904. [Greyfriars gravestone]

MASSON, CHARLES, son of James Masson in Caltonhill, Edinburgh, died on Mount Hindmost Estate, Clarendon, Jamaica, in 1818. [S.56.18]

MASSON, ELIZABETH, daughter of William Masson in Edinburgh, sister of Mary, widow of Charles Lovemore in Jamaica, her heir, 1791. [NRS.S/H]

MATHESON, DONALD, son of Duncan Matheson an advocate in Edinburgh, settled in Macao, China, before 1842. [NRS.S/H]

MATHESON, J., master of the Agincourt of Leith, from Leith to Halifax, Nova Scotia, and Quebec in 1817. [NRS.E504.22.77] [MG]

MATHER, JOHN, a music teacher in Edinburgh, and his wife Marion Frost, a Process of Divorce in 1818. [NRS.CC8.5.36]

MATHIE, ROBERT, a baker on the Shore, Leith, and of the Incorporated Trades of Leith, was appointed Master of the King James Hospital, Leith, on 14 August 1849. [SLR]

MAULE, JOHN, son of Charles Maule in Leith, a merchant in Demerara, died there on 17 October 1798. [AJ.2664] [GC.1159]

MAULE, MARGARET, in Edinburgh, aunt of Hugh Stevenson a merchant in Peru, 1853. [NRS.S/H]

MAURY, PETER, a surgeon, son of Antony Maury, [1760-1846], a confectioner in Edinburgh, died in India. [St Cuthbert's gravestone, Edinburgh]

MAVING, JANET, in Well Close, South Leith, was granted a beggar's badge on 18 February 1794. [SLR]

MAXTON, JOHN, wine merchant, Bank Street, Leith, 1849. [POD]

MEASON, GILBERT, of Mordun, Kirkwall, born 26 February 1725, died on 23 November 1808. [Greyfriars gravestone]

MEEK, ANDREW, a hosier and glover, 43 North Bridge, Edinburgh, in 1849. [POD]

MEIK, PATRICK, in Easter Duddingston, born 1766, died 23 June 1819, husband of Barbara Scott, born 1770, died 13 March 1845, parents of Patrick Meik, born 1810, a Captain of the 31st Bengal Native Infantry, died at Oudh, India, on 17 August 1839. [Duddingston gravestone]

MEIKLE, THOMAS, lately from New York, now in Leith, 1822. [NRS.CS17.1.42]

MEIKLEREID, DAVID, a shipmaster, 41 Shore, Leith, 1849. [POD]

MELDRUM, ROBERT, formerly a Captain in the Service of the East India Company, an inmate of the Lunatic Asylum at Sughtonhall, Edinburgh, died in May 1865. [NRS.PS3.16.427]

MELLIS, Mrs JAMES, from Edinburgh, died at Grove Terrace, Peckham Park, Philadelphia, Pennsylvania, in 1840. [AJ.4856]

MELROSE, COLVIN, a poulterer, 22 Fleshmarket, Edinburgh, 1849. [POD]

MELROSE, WILLIAM, born 17 March 1817 in Edinburgh, son of Andrew Melrose and his wife Margaret Dickson, based in Hong Kong and Macao, China, from 1842 until 1855. [WMC.XIX][NRS.RH4.27.1]

MELVILLE, CHARLES, a writer in Edinburgh, letters,1793. [NRS.59.39.2.82]

MENZIES, ROBERT DRYBURGH, deacon of South Leith parish in 1825. [SLR]; a shipbuilder in Leith, a petitioner in 1828. [SLR]

MERCER, Miss, a milliner and dressmaker, 7 Little King Street, Edinburgh, 1849. [POD]

MERRY, GEORGE, born 1814, eldest son of George Merry a tobacconist in Edinburgh, died in Demerara on 27 February 1839. [SG.8.765]

MERRYLEES, Mrs, a cork-cutter, 48 Water Lane, Edinburgh, 1849. [POD]

METCALF, MARIA, widow of John Marshall, a cutler in Charleston, South Carolina, died in Edinburgh on 15 February 1825. [S.535.128]

METHUEN, JAMES, a fish curer and cooper, 90 Giles Street, Leith, 1849. [POD]

MIDDLEMASS, G., wright, 169 Causeyside, Edinburgh, 1849. [POD]

MILES, ALEXANDER, a shipbuilder, 31 Sandport Street, Leith, 1849. [POD]

MILES, JOHN, a seaman on the Fame of Leith, testament, 1815, Comm. Edinburgh. [NRS]

MILLER, EBENEZER, from Edinburgh, died in Calcutta, India, on 4 December 1797. [AJ.2629]

MILLAR, ELIZABETH, third daughter of Andrew Millar a Writer to the Signet, married Richard James Andrew, from Belize, Honduras, at 11 York Place, Edinburgh, on 13 August 1828. [S.898.530]; parents of a son born in Belize on 29 November 1829. [BM.27.962]

MILLER, or PIERREPOINT, HARRIOT, in Portsmouth, USA, niece and heir of Agnes Miller, widow of John Thompson, a skipper in Leith, in 1830. [NRS.S/H]

MILLER, JAMES, late a merchant in New Providence in the Bahamas, later a resident in Edinburgh, executor of Reeves Fowler, late of New Providence, versus Elizabeth Fowler, daughter of Reeves Fowler, and wife of Dr Mitchell in Virginia, in 1816. [NRS.GD63]

MILLER, JAMES, and Company, timber merchants in Leith, sederunt book, 1826-1827. [NRS.CS96.174]

MILLER, JAMES, a grocer in St Andrew Street, Leith, of the Incorporated Trades of Leith in 1849. [SLR]

MILLER, JANET, versus her husband David Hume a marble polisher in Leith, a Process of Divorce in 1798, [NRS.CC8.5.24]

MILLER, JOHN, born 27 July 1760 in Edinburgh, son of Professor John Miller of Glasgow University, was educated at Glasgow University in 1774, an advocate in 1783, died in Pennsylvania in 1796. [MAGU][CM.11736; 19.11.1796][SM.58.792]

MILLAR, JOHN, born 1808, son of James Miller a merchant in Leith, qualified as a member of the Faculty of Advocates, was appointed Attorney General of the Bahama Islands in 1837, died there that year. [South Leith church window]

MILLER, JOHN, son of James Miller, [1731-1816], a glover, died in Philadelphia, Pennsylvania, on 11 May 1836. [Canongait gravestone, Edinburgh]

MILLER, JOHN WATSON, in Cookshire, Quebec, son and heir of Elizabeth Watson, wife of William Cleugh Miller, a clerk in Edinburgh, who died on 27 January 1851. [NRS.S/H]

MILLER, MARGARET, born 1846, wife of Robert Stein from Edinburgh, died in Pittston, Luzerne County, Pennsylvania, in 1884. [S.12877]

MILLER, MARION, wife of John Grieve, a shoemaker from Edinburgh, then in America, brother and heir of Daniel Miller, a tailor in Edinburgh, in 1807. [NRS.S/H]

MILLER, ROBERT, born 1839 in Edinburgh, an engraver who died in New York on 28 December 1871. [S.8883]

MILLAR, THOMAS, a fisher in Fisherrow, testament, 1803, Comm. Edinburgh. [NRS]

MILLER, WILLIAM, a type founder in Newington, Edinburgh, versus his wife Margaret Duff, a Process of Divorce in 1822. [NRS.CC8.5.41]

MILLER, WILLIAM J., son of James Miller a glover in Edinburgh, died in Woodside, Philadelphia, Pennsylvania, on 20 September 1839. [EEC.19964]

MILLER, WILLIAM HENRY, fourth son of Andrew Miller, a merchant in Edinburgh, and his wife Jane Johnston, died in Barbados in 1857. [St Cuthbert's gravestone, Edinburgh]

MILLER, WILLIAM FORRESTER HARDY, born 1833, died in Portland, Maine, on 26 April 1898. [Old Calton gravestone, Edinburgh]

MILLONS, THOMAS, born 24 April 1830, eldest son of Thomas Millons, and his wife Agnes Noble, in Drumdryan House, Edinburgh, died in Galveston, Texas, on 13 October 1853. [EEC.22510] [Dean gravestone, Edinburgh]

MILLS, NATHAN, born 1749 in Boston, Massachusetts, a printer who died in Edinburgh on 12 October 1824. [S.499.762][TNA.AO12/110/79]

MILNE, HELEN, wife of Robert Fairbairn a joiner from Edinburgh, then in Canada, brother and heir to Charles Milne, a baker in Edinburgh, in 1851. [NRS.S/H]

MILNE, NICOL, in Westminster, Canada, heir to his son Robert Milne, in Wellington Place, Leith, who died on 13 July 1871. [NRS.S/H]

MILNE, PATRICK WILSON, son of Peter Milne, [1815-1887], a baker in Edinburgh, and his wife Isabella MacMillan, [1818-1902], died in Para, Brazil on 14 July 1899. [East Preston Street gravestone]

MINTO, ARCHIBALD B., a cupper of 103 George Street, Edinburgh, 1849. [POD]

MINTO, JAMES, a coppersmith and brazier, 31 Whitefield Place, Edinburgh, 1849. [POD]

MINTO, JOHN, MD, in Edinburgh, father of Archibald Butter Minto who died in New York on 11 December 1869. [S.8250]

MIRES, ANN C., youngest daughter of Henry C. Mires in Leith, married Alexander Waldie, from East Lothian, at the residence of Hon. John Fisher in New York, on 26 September 1867. [S.7555]

MITCHELL, F. G., a wholesale grocer at 10 Shakespeare Square, Edinburgh, 1849. [POD]

MITCHELL, JAMES, youngest son of John Mitchell in Pitt Street, Edinburgh, died in Spanish Town, Jamaica, in 1817. [S.10.17]

MITCHELL, JAMES RITCHIE, a farmer in Tarr, Pennsylvania, brother and heir of Jessie Mitchell of 28 Dundas Street, Edinburgh, who died on 18 March 1867. [NRS.S/H]

MITCHELL, JOHN, in Leith, applied to settle in Canada on 21 January 1819. [TNA.CO384.5.11]

MITCHELL, JOHN, master of the brig Highlander of Leith from Leith bound for Quebec and Montreal in 1833. [LCL.2105]

MITCHELL, MARGARET, wife of William Fabian Meudell, in Belleville, Upper Canada, daughter and heir of George Mitchell, a wright in Edinburgh, who died on 12 May 1831; also, to her mother Helen Anderson, wife of George Mitchell, a wright in Edinburgh, who died on 19 June 1847. [NRS.S/H]

MITCHELL, WILLIAM, a merchant in Edinburgh, father of James Mitchell a Captain in the Service of the East India Company, testament 1789, Comm. Edinburgh. [NRS]

MITCHELL, WILLIAM, born 1838, late of Edinburgh, son of John Mitchell in Yair, Selkirkshire, died in Melbourne, Victoria, Australia, on 27 December 1898. [S.17352]

MITCHELLHILL, CHRISTINA, eldest daughter of Peter Mitchellhill, late of Edinburgh, then in The Grange, Mathoura, New South Wales, Australia, married Philip Bull from Melbourne, Victoria, Australia, at Tweedside, Essenden, near Melbourne, on 20 November 1873. [S.11395]

MOIR, JAMES, born 15 March 1817 in Edinburgh, son of James Moir. and his wife Margaret Stenhouse, a merchant in New York, died there on 7 December 1899. [ANY]

MOFFAT, ANDREW, born 1795 in Duns, Berwickshire, a merchant in Charleston, South Carolina, was naturalised there on 14 February 1820. [NARA.M1183.1]

MOIR, JAMES, born 15 March 1817 in Edinburgh, son of James Moir and his wife Margaret Stenhouse, a merchant in New York, died there on 7 December 1899. [ANY]

MONCRIEFF, ANNIE DILWORTH, born 1824, wife of James Sinclair a printer, both from Edinburgh, died in Nashville, Tennessee, on 7 December 1859. [CM.21617]

MONCREIFF, ARCHIBALD, a merchant in Maryland, died on 6 January 1803, brother of Susan Moncreiff, widow of Reverend William Paul late of St Cuthbert's, Edinburgh, testament, 1818. [NRS.CC8.8.144]

MONEYDAY, WILLIAM, born 1752 in Edinburgh, a merchant in Charleston, South Carolina, on 28 September 1819. [SR.30.9.1819]

MONRO, JOHN CAMPBELL, MD, in South Finch, Canada, heir to his aunt Catherine Monro in Edinburgh, who died on 29 May 1866. [NRS.S/D]

MONTEATH, Mrs AMELIA, widow of Thomas Monteath in Jamaica, heir to her grandfather John Schaw, a merchant in Edinburgh, in 1799. [NRS.S/H]

MONTGOMERY, BARBARA H., wife of John I. Donaldson in New York, daughter and heir to Agnes Greenfield, mother of George Montgomery, a confectioner in Edinburgh, in 1856. [NRS.S/H]

MONTGOMERY, GEORGE HENDERSON, in Columbia, USA, son and heir to Agnes Greenfield, mother of George Montgomery, a confectioner in Edinburgh, in 1856. [NRS.SH]

MONTGOMERY, JOHN, son of Alexander Montgomery a wright in Edinburgh, was apprenticed to William Bruce, an upholsterer in Edinburgh, for seven years on 8 October 1795. [ERA]

MONYPENNY, WILLIAM TANKERVILLE, son of Colonel Alexander Monypenny, was apprenticed to William and John Crawford, merchants in Edinburgh, for five years on 28 November 1799. [ERA]

MOON, D., a billiard table maker of 1 Clyde Street, Edinburgh, in 1849. [POD]

MORGAN, WILLIAM, born 9 December 1836, third son of James Morgan, [1790-1860], and his wife Clementina Kyd, [1805-1881], died in Selma, Arizona, on 28 February 1876. [Dean gravestone, Edinburgh]

MORICE, GEORGE, son of Dr James Morice in Edinburgh, was educated at Marischal College, Aberdeen, in 1854, a minister in New Zealand. [MCA]

MORRISON, DAVID, born 1802, died in America on 10 August 1855. [St Cuthbert's gravestone, Edinburgh]

MORRISON, FRANCIS, from Edinburgh, was naturalised in New York on 5 April 1838. [NY Superior Court Records]

MORRISON, JOHN J., from Leith, an engineer in the Chilean Navy, married Isabella Denholm, daughter of James Denholm a merchant in Glasgow, in Valparaiso, Chile, on 19 July 1861. [S.1964]

MORRISON, MARY, born 1806, wife of David Pringle a carver and gilder from Edinburgh, died in New York on 8 April 1869. [S.8032]

MORISON, ROBERT, a merchant in Havanna, Cuba, later in Edinburgh, son and heir of Robert Morison, a painter in Perth, in 1853. [NRS.S/H]

MORRISON, SOPHIA ELIZA, eldest daughter of David Morrison of the East India Company, married Richard Panton of Jamaica and the University of Cambridge, in Edinburgh on 6 July 1824. [S.470.530]

MORTIMER, T. E., a gunmaker, 97 George Street, Edinburgh, 1849. [POD]

MORTON, ALEXANDER, born 1779 in Leith, a merchant who was naturalised in Charleston, South Carolina, on 18 May 1807. [NARA.M1183.1]

MORTON, GEORGE, born 1790 in Edinburgh, emigrated to America around 1815, an architect in St Louis, Missouri, died in 1865. [WA]

MORTON, WALTER, son of Hugh Morton in Leith, died in St Croix, Danish West Indies, on 5 July 1797. [EEC.416]

MOSSMAN, WILLIAM, a watchmaker from Edinburgh, died in Brooklyn, New York, 4 July 1872. [S.9054]

MOWBRAY, ROBERT, a merchant in Leith, married Milborough Thomson, daughter of John Thomson of Kingston, Jamaica, in Glasgow on 1 June 1803. [EEC.14270]

MOWBRAY, ROBERT C., son of W. Mowbray a merchant in Leith, died in Rome, Italy, on 2 March 1823. [SM.86.648]

MOWBRAY, SEYMOUR, in Killearny, Ireland, heir to his brother Richard Mowbray a farmer from Edinburgh, then in Ottowa, Canada, in 1860. [NRS.S/H]

MOWBRAY, WILLIAM, deacon of South Leith parish in 1825. [SLR]; a merchant in Leith, a petitioner in 1828. [SLR]

MOXEY, LOUIS WHITE, son of John Gray Moxey from Edinburgh, died in Philadelphia, Pennsylvania, on 18 August 1841. [EEC.20268]

MUIR, JAMES, born 1794, from Edinburgh, died in Newark, New Jersey, in 1876. [S.10162]

MUIR, JANET, in Well's Close, South Leith, was granted a beggar's badge on 18 February 1794. [SLR]

MUIR, JOHN, jr., a writer in Edinburgh, was admitted as a burgess and guilds-brother of Dunfermline, Fife, on 5 May 1791. [DM]

MUIR, PETER, a bow-maker in Archer's Hall, Edinburgh, 1849. [POD]

MUIR, WILLIAM CHARLES, son of Charles B. Muir and his wife Robina Frances Hunter, died in Montreal, Quebec, on 2 February 1860. [Canongait gravestone]

MUIRHEAD, JAMES, born 1793 in Edinburgh, an accountant in Charleston, South Carolina, was naturalised there on 27 August 1813. [NARA.M1183.1]

MUNRO, DANIEL, master of the Mary of Leith trading between Greenock and Savannah, Georgia, in 1810; between Greenock and Pictou, Nova Scotia, in 1817; and between Leith and Quebec in 1819. [NRS.E504.15.90/115; E504.22.84]

MUNRO, DAVID, master of the Mary of Leith trading between Leith and Pictou, Nova Scotia, in 1820. [NRS.E504.22.89]

MUNRO, Reverend HARRY, born 1730, a missionary of the Society for the Propagation of the Gospel, emigrated to New York in 1765, late Rector of St Peter's, Albany, New York, a Loyalist army chaplain, settled in Bannockburn, Stirlingshire, by 1788, died in Edinburgh on 30 May 1801. [St Cuthbert gravestone, Edinburgh] [TNA.AO12.24.36, etc] [NRS.RD3.289.717] [EMA.47] [FPA.304/327]

MUNRO, JAMES, son of John Munro a merchant in Edinburgh, died in China in January 1799. [AJ.2652]

MUNRO, JAMES GORDON, son of James Gordon Munro of Saxe Coburg Place, Edinburgh, died in Georgetown, Demerara, in 1851. [S.11.2.1852]

MUNRO, WILLIAM, a slater in Broughton Street, Edinburgh, father of William Munro, born 1764, died in Guadaloupe, French West Indies, on 26 March 1885. [S.13030]

MURDOCH, JOHN, and his wife Flora Ritchie, parents of David Ritchie Murdoch, born 1859, died in Montreal Quebec, on 12 November 1894. [St Cuthbert's gravestone, Edinburgh]

MURRAY, ALEXANDER JOHN, born 1813, second son of David Murray an accountant in Edinburgh, died in Berbice in August 1837. [AJ.4691]

MURRAY, BASIL HAMILTON, born 1823, son of Sir James Murray of Philiphaugh, a Lieutenant of the 43rd Regiment of Light Infantry on the Bengal Establishment, in India, died in Edinburgh on 1 April 1849. [Greyfriars gravestone]

MURRAY, CHRISTIANA, daughter of George Murray, a merchant, married William Gordon of Evie, in Lauriston Place, Edinburgh, in 1820. [SM.85]

MURRAY, GEORGE, son of William Murray a merchant in New Street, Canongait, died in Antigua in September 1798. [EA][SM.61.72]

MURRAY, JAMES WOLFE, born in Louisbourg, Nova Scotia, in 1759, son of Alexander Murray, died in 1836. [Greyfriars gravestone, Edinburgh]

MURRAY, JANE, wife of Alexander Schawfield a physician in Virginia, heir to his grandfather John Schawfield, a merchant in Edinburgh, in 1799. [NRS.S/H]

MURRAY, JOHN, son of John Murray, [1764-1820, a merchant, and his wife Janet Shaw, [1779-1859], died in Ewake, USA, aged 72. [South Leith gravestone]

MURRAY, JOHN, an accountant in Edinburgh, brother and heir of Andrew Murray and Gilbert Murray, both in Jamaica, in 1837. [NRS.S/H]

MURRAY, WILLIAM, son of David Murray a writer, was apprenticed to Elphinstone Balfour a bookseller in Edinburgh, in 1797. [ERA]

MURRAY, WILLIAM R., born 1820, eldest son of John Murray and his wife Anne Jane Borland, an assistant surgeon in the Service of the East India Company, died in Dhoolia, India, on 16 January 1850. [St Cuthbert's gravestone, Edinburgh]

MURRAY, WILLIAM, a farmer in New York, son and heir of John Murray, a baker in Edinburgh, in 1857. [NRS.S/H]

MUSGRAVE, W. T., a portrait painter, 32 Royal Circus, Edinburgh, 1849. [POD]

MUSHET, JAMES, a haberdasher, 33 Nicolson Street, Edinburgh, 1849. [POD]

MYLNE, PETER, a baker in the Cowgait of Edinburgh, versus his wife Elspeth Clyne, a Process of Divorce in 1803. [NRS.CC8.5.20]

MYLNE, WILLIAM, formerly a merchant in Leith, died at Lothian Cottage, Dunnville, Upper Canada, on 1 October 1845. [EEC.21264]

NAPIER, J., a printer's lead-caster, 13 West Nicolson Street, Edinburgh, 1849. [POD]

NASMITH, ALEXANDER, born 1758, died in 1840. [St Cuthbert's gravestone, Edinburgh]

NAYSMYTH, CHARLES JAMES, a merchant in Calcutta, India, son of James Naysmyth, a goldsmith in Edinburgh, who died on 17 March 1855. [NRS.S/H]

NASMITH, WILLIAM, born 1812, a blacksmith in Blair Street, Edinburgh, with his wife Christian born 1814, and sons John born 1840, and Alexander born 1842, emigrated to South Australia in 1848. [BPP.11.172]

NAISMITH, WILLIAM, born 1826, second son of William Naismith of 2 Causewayside, Edinburgh, died in Brooklyn, New York, on 27 August 1861. [S.1981]

NAPIER, ARCHIBALD, from Tobago, married Ann Stirling, daughter of Sir John Stirling of Glovat, in Edinburgh, on 24 December 1812. [SM.75.77]; he died in Edinburgh on 16 February 1822. [DPCA.1023]

NEILL, WILLIAM, born 9 March 1816 in Edinburgh, son of John Neill, died in Jamaica in 1838. [Calton gravestone, Edinburgh]

NEILSON, CHRISTINA, married Dr Shaw from Jamaica, in Edinburgh on 24 October 1817. [S.37.17]

NEILSON, JAMES, son of Gilbert Neilson a merchant in Edinburgh, died in Baltimore, Maryland, on 4 July 1821. [DPCA][EA]

NELSON, THOMAS S., late of the National Bank of Scotland in Edinburgh, father of a son born at 295 South Street, Brooklyn, New York, on 17 March 1871. [S.8633]

NESBIT, JAMES, born in Edinburgh, was naturalised in South Carolina on 18 June 1812. [S.C.Circuit Court Journal 10.79]

NESS, DAVID, a marble cutter, 15 Leith Walk, Edinburgh, in 1849. [POD]

NEWBIGGING, JAMES, a house painter, 31 Candlemaker Row, Edinburgh, 1849. [POD]

NEWBIGGING, JOHN, a gold beater in the Canongait, versus his wife Margaret Walker, a Process of Divorce in 1830. [NRS.CC8.6.166]

NEWLAND, ALEXANDER, son of John Newland in Edinburgh, probate 4 December 1809, New Jersey. [NJSA.10593G]

NEWLAND, ANTHONY, born 1769 in Edinburgh, a merchant in New York by 1808, died in Newark, New Jersey, on 29 November 189. [ANY]

NEWLAND, JESSIE, born 1858, daughter of John Newland, died in New York on 11 May 1861. [S.1866]

NEWLANDS, MARGARET, wife of John Chalmers, a labourer in Edinburgh, brother and heir of John Newlands in Jamaica, in 1812. [NRS.S/H]

NEWLANDS, MATTHEW, a ropemaker in Edinburgh, versus his wife Agnes Brownlee, a Process of Divorce in 1822. [NRS.CC8.6.133]

NEWTON, JOHN, master of the Royal Bounty of Leith, whaling in the Davis Straits in 1799, [AJ.2689]; a shipmaster in Leith, testament, 1824, Comm. Edinburgh. [NRS]

NEWTON, J., a hat manufacturer, Tennis Court, Edinburgh, in 1849. [POD]

NEWTON, W., master of the Urania of Leith from Leith bound for Quebec and Montreal in 1820. [NRS.E504.22.91]

NICOL, ALEXANDER, born 1823, third son of John Nicol a builder in Lauriston, Edinburgh, died in Kingston, North Carolina, on 6 October 1884. [S.12920]

NICOL, ROBERT, in St Thomas, Upper Canada, son and heir of William Nicol, son and heir of William Nicol, a brazier in Fountainbridge, Edinburgh, who died on 12 March 1830. [NRS.S/H]

NICHOLSON, RICHARD, in Brooklyn, New York, son and heir of Mary Fawcett, widow of John Nicholson, a tailor from Edinburgh later in New York, died on 6 December 1865. [NRS.S/H]

NICHOLSON, WILLIAM, [1784-1844], of the Royal Scottish Academy in Edinburgh, and his wife Maria Lamb, [1804-1873], parents of Agnes Reid Nicholson, who ded in Washington, USA, on 27 November 1881. [St Cuthbert's gravestone, Edinburgh]

NIMMO, AMELIA, wife of Robert Carnegy, MD, a surgeon in Edinburgh, died at 1 Forth Street, Edinburgh, on 19 September 1822. [SM.90.632]

NIMMO, WILLIAM, son of John Nimmo a baker in Leith, was apprenticed to James Welsh, a baker in Edinburgh, for six years, on 27 March 1800. [ERA]

NISBET, ANDREW, son of Robert a tailor in the Canongait, was apprenticed to George Gregory a tin plate worker in Edinburgh, for seven years on 5 September 1799. [ERA]

NISBET, ELIZABETH ISABELLA, wife of Andrew Fraser in Illinois, heir to her nephew Thomas Nisbet in 5 Gayfield Square, Edinburgh, who died on 11 July 1862. [NRS.S/H]

NIVEN, JOHN, a merchant, married Mary Spalding, widow of Dr Alexander Spalding late in Port Maria, West Indies, in Leith on 15 September 1824. [S.491.698][DPCA.1156]

NOEL, ELIZABETH, daughter of Joseph Noel, married George McCartney, MD, Professor of Anatomy and Physiology, at 40 Hanover Street, Edinburgh, on 13 April 1829. [S.968.248]

NORMAND, JOSEPH, in Worcester, Massachusetts, grandson and heir of Joseph Normand, a wright from Edinburgh, later in America, who died in October 1852. [NRS.S/H]

NORRIE, DAVID, born 1837, late of the Royal High School of Edinburgh, husband of Catherine ...., died in 682 Osgood Street, Chicago, Illinois, on 9 January 1899. [S.17343]

NORRIS, JAMES, master of the <u>Rambler of Leith</u> from Tobermory to Prince Edward Island in 1806. [PAPEI][PANS]; from Thurso, Caithness, and Stromness, Orkney, with passengers, was shipwrecked near the Bay of Bulls, Newfoundland on 29 October 1807. [AJ.3119/3129[IJ.13.11.1807; 25.12.1807][IC.13.11.1807]

NOTMAN, D., a mason, 3 Young Street, Edinburgh, in 1849. [POD]

NOTMAN, JOHN, born 22 July 1810 in Edinburgh, son of David Notman and his wife Mary Christie, an architect who emigrated to Philadelphia, Pennsylvania, in 1831, died n 3 March 1865. [AP]

NOTMAN, MARY JOLLY, daughter of John Notman from Edinburgh, widow of Thomas Thorp, died in Patterson, New Jersey, on 20 March 1877. [EC.28867][S.10519]

NOTMAN, PETER, born 14 August 1820 in Edinburgh, emigrated to America in 1833, an underwriter in New York, died in Brooklyn, NY, on 26 October 1893. [AP]

NOURSE, WALTER, son of John Nourse and his wife Elizabeth ……., was born on 11 August 1797 and baptised in the church of St John the Evangelist in Edinburgh on 24 September 1797. [NRS.CH12.3.26.2]

OGILVIE, ALEXANDER MILNE, son of Robert Ogilvie in Leith, died in New York on 26 April 1847. [EEC.21530]

OGILVIE, JAMES, from Leith, died 1790 in Georgia. [Georgia Gazette, 19.8.1790]

OGILVIE, JAMES, a merchant in Edinburgh, father of Archibald Ogilvie who died in Westchester, New York, on 13 December 1866. [S.7306]

OGILVIE, ROBERT, a merchant in Leith, father of John Ogilvie in Holland, the Netherlands, 1859. [NRS.S/H]

OLD, WILLIAM, a labourer from Edinburgh, bound via Greenock for Canada in 1815. [TNA.CO385.2]

OLIPHANT, ALEXANDER, son of Charles Oliphant a merchant, was apprenticed to William Gordon, a bookseller in Edinburgh, for five years, on 15 September 1796. [ERA]

OLIPHANT, DAVID, a printer from Leith, with Clementina his wife and three children, applied to emigrate to Canada in 1815. [TNA.CO385/2]; born 1770, a printer in Leith, wife Clementina McKenzie born 1776, David born 1800, William born 1803, and Jean born 1798, emigrated via Greenock to Upper Canada in 1815. [TNA.AO3]

OLIPHANT, DAVID, son of James Oliphant a goldsmith and jeweller in Edinburgh, a painter in Charleston, South Carolina by 1787, there in 1806. [NRS.CS17.1.6/196; CS17.1.7.345; CS17.1.25/340]

OLIPHANT, DAVID, in Jamaica, nephew and heir of John Oliphant, a merchant in Leith, in 1809. [NRS.S/H]

OLIPHANT, DAVID, son of David Oliphant a merchant in Edinburgh, died in Jamaica on 23 September 1811. [SM.74.316]

OLIPHANT, FRANCIS, born 1785, a merchant in Edinburgh, died on 28 May 1840, husband of Euphemia Grove, born 1790, died 1875. [St Cuthbert's gravestone, Edinburgh]

OLIPHANT, JANE, eldest daughter of William Oliphant the Customs Collector of Leith, married Richard Pechard jr. a merchant in St John's, Newfoundland, on 9 June 1834. [AJ.4517]

OLIPHANT, JEMIMA, daughter of James Oliphant a jeweller in Edinburgh and his wife Jean Nevay, wife of John Morison, dead by June 1804. [NRS.CC8.8.136]

OLIPHANT, JOHN, a merchant in Leith, dead by 1809, uncle of David Oliphant in Jamaica. [NRS.S/H]

OLIPHANT, WILLIAM, in Leith, father of Jane Oliphant who married Richard Perchard jr., a merchant in St John's, Newfoundland, there on 11 May 1834. [Royal Gazette and Newfoundland Advertiser, 20.5.1834]

OLIPHANT, WILLIAM, born 1844, son of Walter Oliphant a publisher in Edinburgh, died in Clifford, Ontario, in 1885. [S.13038]

OMAN, CHARLES, eldest son of Charles Oman in West Register Street, Edinburgh, died on Trinity Estate, St Mary's, Jamaica, on 18 November 1818. [S.106.19]

O'NEILL, JOHN, in Roxbury, Boston, Massachusetts, heir to his uncle Anthony O'Neill, a statuarymaker in Edinburgh, who died on 7 September 1849. [NRS.S/H]

ORKNEY, JOHN, born 1787 in Edinburgh, died in North Carolina on 1 February 1872. [Washington Presbyterian gravestone, Beaufort County, N.C.]

ORMISTON, GEORGE, an ironmonger, 166 Rose Street, Edinburgh, in 1849. [POD]

ORMOND, HELEN, daughter of John Ormond in Leith, died in Verdura, Florida, on 27 August 1841. [EEC.20273]

ORMOND, RUSSELL, daughter of John Ormond in Leith, wife of Joseph Chaires in Tallahassee, died in Verdura, Florida, on 29 August 1841. [EEC.20273]

ORMSTED, JORGEN CAPPELEN, born 1780 in Dram, Norway, a merchant in Edinburgh in 1803. [EBR.SL.115]

ORPHOOT, JOHN, born 1771, died 2 June 1849, husband of Joan Clark Henderson, born 1792, died 8 January 1860. [St Cuthbert's gravestone]

ORR, JOHN, born 1813, died in Montreal, Quebec, on 20 April 1856, [New Calton gravestone, Edinburgh]

ORR, Captain SAMUEL, son of James Orr a merchant in Leith, died in Kingston, Jamaica, on 9 July 1813. [SM.75.959] [EA]

ORR, THOMAS, born in 1809, eldest son of Thomas Orr a timber merchant in Edinburgh, 'for many years in Havanna, Cuba', died in New Orleans, Louisiana, on 10 June 1870. [S.8413]

ORR, WILLIAM, in Edinburgh, applied to settle in Canada on 28 February 1815. [NRS.RH9]

ORROCK, JAMES, a dentist, 7 Abercromby Place, Edinburgh, 1849. [POD]

OSWALD, JOHN, from Edinburgh, died in West Troy, Albany County, New York, on 15 November 1845. [EEC.21286]

OVENSTONE, W., a tea and coffee dealer, 46 Quality Street, Edinburgh, 1849. [POD]

OWEN, THOMAS, born 1774, a surgeon who died in Madras, India, on 14 January 1833. [St Cuthbert's gravestone]

PANTAR, CHARLES, in Edinburgh, versus his wife Mary Buchanan, a Process of Divorce in 1825. [NRS.CC8.6.145]

PANTON, GEORGE, a mercantile agent and a tenant in the Bush, Leith, in 1811. [LD]

PARKE, ALEXANDER, French teacher, 17 Dundas Street, Edinburgh, 1849. [POD]

PARK, ANDREW, elder of South Leith parish in 1825. [SLR]; a wood merchant in Leith, a petitioner in 1828; an elder on 1 October 1843. [SLR]

PARKER, M., an oil merchant, 2 Crown Street, Edinburgh, 1849. [POD]

PATERSON, GEORGE, from Leith, of the Royal Navy, testament, 1826, Comm. Edinburgh. [NRS]

PATERSON, ISABEL, married John Bruce, late of Grenada, in 41 Great King Street, Edinburgh, on 17 April 1827. [BM.21.772]

PATERSON, MARGARET LINTON, daughter of William Paterson, [1811-1875], a merchant in Edinburgh, and wife of James N. Adam, died in Buffalo, New York, on 28 August 1894. [St Cuthbert's gravestone, Edinburgh]

PATTERSON, ROBERT, in Demerara, father of John Winter Patterson, born 1815, who was educated at Edinburgh Academy from 1824 until 1828. [EAR]

PATERSON, THOMAS, a ropemaker from Leith, later in Baltimore, Maryland, 1779. [NRS.CS16.1.175]; a sasine, 1810. [NRS.RS27.250/260]

PATERSON, WALKER, and Company, merchants in Leith, sederunt book, 1819-1821. [NRS.CS96.897]

PATTISON, EDWARD, from Edinburgh, a die maker at Lima Mint in Peru, married Carolina Juanita Maria, youngest daughter of Luis

Francisco Vaslin, a merchant in Lima, on 5 February 1868; he died in Lima on 6 May 1868, while she died there on 5 November 1868. [S.7690/7761/7919]

PATISON, JOHN, Town Clerk of Leith, 1793. [SLR]

PATON, ANDREW ARCHIBALD, in Brussels, Belgium, son of Andrew Paton a saddler in Edinburgh, who died on 13 October 1852. [NRS.S/H]

PATON, WILLIAM, born 1818 in Edinburgh, settled as a merchant in New York in 1832, died on 25 September 1890. [ANY]

PATTULLO, JAMES, and his wife Jane Morrison Leburn, parents of James Leburn Pattullo, born in Edinburgh on 12 November 1853, was educated at Edinburgh University, a minister in New Zealand from 1883. [F.7.605]

PAUL, JOHN ERSKINE, second son of Robert Paul a banker in Edinburgh, died on his passage from New York on 30 January 1850. [W.1083]

PAXTON, JOHN, an auctioneer at 6 Royal Exchange, Edinburgh, in 1849. [POD]

PEACOCK, ADAM, tobacconist, 54 the Shore, Leith, 1849. [POD]

PEACOCK, THOMAS, born 1841, son of Thomas Peacock, MD, died in Hoprig, Emmet County, Iowa, on 6 February 1903. [Liberton gravestone, Edinburgh]

PEATTIE, ALEXANDER, son of George Peattie a bookseller, was apprenticed to Alexander Bruce, a wright in Edinburgh, for six years, on 31 January 1799. [ERA]

PECK, JAMES, a lithographic printer, 6 George Street, Edinburgh, 1849. [POD]

PENDER, JAMES BAILLIE, son of Thomas Pender the Deputy Collector of Stamps in North Britain, was apprenticed to Andrew Wood a surgeon apothecary in Edinburgh for five years on 31 October 1799. [ERA]

PENDRIGH, JOHN, born 1797, died 27 November 1831, husband of Isabella Miller, born 1800, died 6 November 1870. [Duddingston gravestone]

PENDRICH, JOHN, baker at 47 Fountainbridge, Edinburgh, in 1849. [POD]

PENNYCUICK, JOHN, spirit dealer, 76 Causeyside, Edinburgh, 1849. [POD]

PENNYCOOK, ROBERT, in Westmoreland, Jamaica, nephew and heir of Robert Fullerton in Edinburgh, in 1823. [NRS.S/H]

PENTLAND, Y. J., a cooper, 23 Spence Place, Leith, 1849. [POD]

PERRY, Mrs AMELIA, from Montreal, Quebec, died in West Richmond Street, Edinburgh, on 21 August 1827. [EA.6653.559]

PERRIE, DAVID, Deacon of the Wrights of South Leith, a letter, 1829. [SLR]

PERRIE, Mrs ISABELLA, from Charleston, South Carolina, died in Edinburgh on 20 October 1823. [SM.92.768]

PETER, Sir JOHN, born 1745, late British Consul General in the Netherlands, died 19 June 1826. [Greyfriars gravestone]

PETERKIN, ALEXANDER, in Newington, Edinburgh, a summons in 1825. [NRS.SC111.5.1825.41]

PETERKIN, J., a smith, 61 Canongate, Edinburgh, 1849. [POD]

PETRIE, JOHN, son of John Petrie a printer, was apprenticed to James Johnston, an engraver in Edinburgh, for seven years, on 11 May 1797. [ERA]

PETRIE, THOMAS JAMES HOYGHUE, born in 1813, son of William Petrie, MD, a surgeon in the Royal Navy, in Leith, died in Kingston, Jamaica, in November 1827. [EA.6697.79]

PEW, ALEXANDER, a block-maker and pump maker in Leith, 1777, [NRS.CS228.P5.17.2]; dead by 1819, father of Alexander Pew in Jamaica, in 1819. [NRS.S/H]; Alexander Pew jr, died at Annetto Bay, Jamaica, in 1820. [BM.8.240]

PEW, ALEXANDER, youngest son of Alexander Pew in Leith, died at Anetto Bay, Jamaica, in 1820. [BM.8.240][SM]

PHILIP, ALEXANDER, son of Charles Philip a merchant in Leith, was apprenticed to John Watson, a merchant in Leith, for five years, on 6 April 1797. [ERA]

PHILIPS, ROBERT, a grocer in Leith Walk, Edinburgh, a summons in 1825. [NRS.SC11.5.1825.41]

PIKE, WILLIAM, 37 Princes Street, Edinburgh, 1849. [POD]

PILLANS, ELIZABETH, wife of Henry Grant in South Carolina, daughter and heir to William Pillans, a shipmaster in Leith, 1795. [NRS.S/H]

PIPER, Count CHARLES FREDRIC, born 1781 in Stockholm, Sweden, arrived in Edinburgh in 1803. [EBR.SL.115]

PIRIE, Reverend JOHN, from Edinburgh, married Fanny Maria Fraser, youngest daughter of Reverend Alexander Fraser in New York, in Kenmore, Perthshire, on 12 June 1861. [S.1867]

PIRIE, ..., a sailor aboard the Raith of Leith was captured by the French, on the return voyage from Greenland, and imprisoned in Dunkirk, Flanders, in 1794. [PL.296]

PITBLADDO, THOMAS, born 18 April 1837, son of James Pitbladdo and his wife Margaret......, in Edinburgh, died in Jamaica on 23 February 1877. [Montego Bay gravestone, Jamaica]

PITCAIRN, ALEXANDER, a merchant in Edinburgh, was appointed attorney for the children of Ralph Bowie in York, Pennsylvania, in 1785, [NRS.RD3.305.1153]; in 1820 this was changed to David Pitcairn in Edinburgh, as their factor. [NRS.RD5.183.607]

PITCAIRN, JOHN, MD, born in 1800, son of William Pitcairn, died in Java, Dutch East Indies, in August 1840. [St Cuthbert's gravestone]

PLAYFAIR, THOMAS, an architect in 17 Great Stuart Street, Edinburgh, in 1849. [POD]

PLENDERLEITH, ALICE, widow of James Grant a merchant in Edinburgh, died in George Street, Edinburgh, on 24 November 1819. [SM.85]

PLENDERLEATH, ROBERT, son of Reverend David Plenderleath, born 1759, a merchant, died on 24 November 1837. [Greyfriars gravestone]

PLEYDALL, JOHN, a merchant, son of Samuel Pleydall, MD, in Jamaica, died in Edinburgh on 13 March 1807. [SM.69.318]

PLUMMER, WILLIAM, son of Andrew Plummer a butcher, was apprenticed to Andrew Plummer a butcher in Edinburgh, for six years on 10 September 1795. [ERA]

POLLOCK, GRAY, born 18 June 1802, son of Reverend John Pollock and his wife Margaret Dickson, died on 25 June 1836 in Julapa, Mexico. [F.3.413] [New Calton gravestone, Edinburgh]

POLLOCK, HUGH, son of Hugh Pollock a wine cooper in Leith, was apprenticed to James Thomson, a baker in Edinburgh, for five years on 16 June 1791. [ERA]

POLLOCK, WILLIAM, of Whitehall, late of the 60th Regiment, died in Edinburgh on 18 September 1822. [SM.90.632]

PONTON, ALEXANDER, a distillery worker in Edinburgh, versus Jean Tweedie, they married in 1786, separated in 1788, and divorced in 1791, a Process of Divorce in 1791. [NRS.CC8.5.20]

PORTEOUS, ALEXANDER, a currier, 31 Rose Street Lane, Edinburgh, 1849. [POD]

PORTEOUS, WILLIAM, son of William Porteous in Edinburgh, was apprenticed to Innes and Wallace, gunsmiths in Edinburgh, for five years on 5 October 1797. [ERA]

PORTER, FRANCES GREIG, in Australia, daughter and heir of Henry Porter, a printer in Edinburgh, in 1856. [NRS.S/H]

PORTER, HENRY, in North America, son and heir of Henry Porter, a printer in Edinburgh, in 1856. [NRS.S/H]

POTTER, ANNE MOIR, born 11 March 1838 in New Orleans, Louisiana, daughter of Robert Potter and his wife Grace Fraser from Edinburgh, died in Edinburgh on 18 May 1889. [Greyfriars gravestone, Edinburgh]

POTTER, GRACE FRASER, born 4 August 1836 in Edinburgh, daughter of Robert Potter and his wife Grace Fraser from Edinburgh, died in New Orleans, Louisiana, on 11 September 1838. [Greyfriars gravestone, Edinburgh]

PRATT, ROBERT, in Sherriff Brae, South Leith, was granted a beggar's badge on 18 February 1794. [SLR]

PRIMROSE, JOHN WILSON, in South Minneapolis, Minnesota, heir to his aunt Sarah Primrose in Edinburgh who died between 1838 and 1843. [NRS.S/H]

PRIMROSE, NICOL, youngest son of Robert Primrose a surgeon in Musselburgh, Midlothian, settled in Charleston, South Carolina, as a merchant in 1780, was naturalised there on 27 February 1783, died there on 13 November 1796. [EEC.12303] [SCA]

PRINGLE, BILLIE, a merchant in Leith, 1793. [NRS.CS97.112.16]

PRINGLE, MARGARET, daughter of William Pringle and grand-daughter of John Pringle in 40 North Richmond Street, Edinburgh, died in New York on 27 September 1871. [S.803]

PROCTOR, A., a plumber and gasfitter, 5 Church Lane, Edinburgh, 1849. [POD]

PROPHET, THOMAS, a fish dealer in Edinburgh, versus his wife Mary Ross, a Process of Divorce in 1826. [NRS.CC8.6.169]

PROUDFOOT, THOMAS, born 1790, a baker in Portobello, Mid Lothian, died 3 October 1854, husband of Mary Davidson, born 2 August 1794, died 13 October 1862. [Duddingston gravestone]

PROUDFOOT, WILLIAM, born 1752, a farmer at Inveresk, died 21 April 1824, husband of Marion Stevenson, 1758, died 15 March 1810. [Duddingston gravestone]

PURDIE, JOHN, a nurseryman, seedsman and florist, Stanwell Lodge, Edinburgh, 1849. [POD]

PURDIE, THOMAS, a merchant in Edinburgh, grandfather of Eliza De Thorais in Moscow, Russia, in 1855. [NRS.S/H]

PYOTT, ARCHIBALD, third son of James Pyott of the Leith Ropery Company, died in Philadelphia, Pennsylvania, on 22 August 1845. [EEC.21243][W.607]

PYOTT, JAMES, a grocer and spirit dealer, 1 Charlotte Street, Leith, 1849. [POD]

QUA, ALEXANDER, born 1833 in Paris, Canada West, died in Edinburgh on 11 August 1862. [Dean gravestone]

RAEBURN, Captain JOHN, of 14 Hermitage Place, Edinburgh, father of William Raeburn, born 1865, was drowned at Port Oliva in South America in 1881. [S.12027]

RAIT, ROBERT, born 1806 in Edinburgh, a jeweller in New York from 1833 until 1866, died on 1 February 1869. [ANY]

RALSTON, A. D., stay and corset maker, 10 Buccleuch Street, Edinburgh, 1849. [POD]

RAMAGE, DICK, son of Alexander Ramage a shoemaker in Leith, was apprenticed to William Sibbald and Company, merchants in Leith, on 1 November 1798. [ERA]

RAMAGE, JOHN, a shipmaster in Leith, testament, 1806, Comm. Edinburgh. [NRS]

RAMSAY, ALEXANDER, born 1754 in Edinburgh, was educated in Edinburgh and in Dublin, a physician and an anatomist, settled in America in 1801, died at Parsonfield, Maine, on 24 November 1824. [SA][WA]

RAMSAY, ANDREW, son of Captain MacNaughton a skipper in Leith, was apprenticed to Andrew Hunter, a merchant in Leith, for five years, on 25 October 1792. [ERA]

RAMSAY, DAVID, deacon of South Leith parish in 1825. [SLR]; a merchant in Leith, a petitioner in 1828. [SLR]

RAMSAY, DANIEL, of Fala, Mid Lothian, a merchant in Edinburgh, died in 1824, husband of Catherine Hamilton, born 1762, died in 1825. [St John's gravestone, Edinburgh]

RAMSAY, JOHN, from Leith, a Lieutenant of the Royal Navy, testament, 1806, Comm. Edinburgh. [NRS]

RAMSAY, MACNAUGHTON, a shipmaster in Leith, inventory, 1812, Comm. Edinburgh. [NRS.SC70.1.6.89]

RAMSAY, ROBERT, in Montreal, Quebec, brother and heir of David Ramsay, a merchant in Leith, in 1850. [NRS.S/H]

RANKINE, JAMES, son of John Rankine a skinner at the Water of Leith, was apprenticed to George Skelton, a clock and watchmaker in Edinburgh, for seven years, on 24 February 1791. [ERA]

RANKIN, ROBERT, a merchant and grocer in Edinburgh between 1821 and 1834, absconded to New York, later in Savannah, Georgia, and possibly in Virginia. [NRS.CS46.1835]

RATTRAY, AGNES, from Edinburgh, in New York, a sasine, 6 August 1829. [NRS.RS.Edinburgh.34.12]

RATTRAY, JAMES, master of the schooner Lady Ross of Leith, a bond of caution, 1803. [NRS.CS271.785]

REID, ALEXANDER, born 1777 in Edinburgh, a watchmaker who was naturalised in Charleston, South Carolina, on 27 September 1813. [NARA.M1183.1]

REID, ALEXANDER M., born 1845, son of Adam F. Reid, [1811-1853], died on 9 April 1879 and was buried in Philadelphia, Pennsylvania. [Dean gravestone, Edinburgh]

REID, Dr ALEXANDER, from Hill Place, Edinburgh, died in Xenia, Green County, Ohio, in 1854. [S.7.10.1854]

REID, DAVID WILLIAM, in New York, grandson and heir of Peter Reid MD in Edinburgh who died on 8 June 1836; and heir to Isobel Miller, widow of John Mackenzie, a glazier in Edinburgh, who died on 27 August 1846; also, heir to John Mackenzie, a glazier in Edinburgh; who died on 1 December 1849; and to his grandmother Christian Arnot, wife of Dr Peter Reid in Edinburgh, who died on 15 December 1851. [NRS.S/H]

REID, HELEN, born 21 April 1811, daughter of Sir James John Reid and his wife Mary Threshie, widow of William Keir an advocate, died in Brantford, Ontario, on 16 October 1884. [Grayfriars gravestone, Edinburgh]

REID, JAMES, second son of Alexander Reid, South Castle Street, Edinburgh, died in St Dorothy's, Jamaica, on 14 January 1822. [DPCA]

REID, JOHN, son of John Reid a wright in Potter Row, Edinburgh, was apprenticed to James Watson a painter in Edinburgh, for six years, on 9 December 1790. [ERA]

REID, JOHN, son of Matthew Reid a plumber, was apprenticed to Alexander Clark, a painter in Edinburgh, for six years, on 14 November 1793. [ERA]

REID, JOHN, a weaver in Broughton Loan, Edinburgh, was accused of theft and reset in 1815. [NRS.AD14.15.25]

REID, JOHN, formerly a minister in Borthwick, died in Sydney, New South Wales, Australia, on 4 April 1864. [AJ.6076]

REID, Dr PETER, in Edinburgh, father of Dr Laurence Reid who died in New York on 4 February 1874. [EC.27892]

REID, PETER, born 1802 in Leith, died in Halifax, Nova Scotia, in June 1840. [Colonial Pearl, 20.6.1840]

REID, THOMAS, from Leith, Captain of the barque *Aries*, died in Rio de Janeiro, Brazil, on 19 January 1868. [S.7665]

REID, Reverend WILLIAM, of Edinburgh, married Clara Violet Hill, daughter of William Hill of New Orleans, Louisiana, at 4 Forres Street, Edinburgh, on 31 October 1854. [EEC.22653]

REID, Dr WILLIAM, in Edinburgh, father of Peter Boswell Reid who died in New York on 23 January 1874. [EC.27882]

RENTON, HENRY, from Kelso, Roxburghshire, a minister in Jamaica, son and heir of William Renton, a merchant in Edinburgh, in 1855. [NRS.S/H]

RENTON, W., a grocer and spirit dealer, 36 Tolbooth Wynd, Leith, 1849. [POD]

REOCH. JAMES, born 1757 in Leith, a Provost of Leith and Master of the Merchant Company there, an elder on 1 October 1843; died in November 1845. [South Leith gravestone]

RESTON, Reverend JOHN, formerly of the Relief Church in Edinburgh, died in Wilmington, North Carolina, on 11 September 1829. [BM.27.134] [S.14.1016] [AJ.4266]

REYNOLDS, R., master of the William Young of Leith from Leith with passengers bound for the Cape of Good Hope, South Africa, Van Diemen's Land, [Tasmania], and Sydney, New South Wales, Australia, in September 1828. [S.XII.894] [AJ.4261]

RICHARD, ALEXANDER, son of John Richard of the Stamp Office, was apprenticed to John Walker, a surgeon apothecary in Edinburgh, for five years, on 6 February 1800. [ERA]

RICHARDSON, ANN, wife of George Hogg a wright in America, daughter and heir of John Richardson, a smith in Edinburgh, 1802. [NRS.S/H]

RICHARDSON, GEORGE, son of William Richardson a clock and watchmaker, was apprenticed to Thomas Reid a clock and watchmaker in Edinburgh for six years, on 12 October 1795. [ERA]

RICHARDSON, JAMES, a sugar refiner, Calton Place, Edinburgh, 1849. [POD]

RICHARDSON, THOMAS, from Edinburgh, a carpenter in Charleston, South Carolina, probate 7 April 1792, S.C.

RICHARDSON, WILLIAM BROWN, born in 1840, youngest son of Francis Richardson and his wife Christian in Edinburgh, died at the Potosi Mines in Venezuela, on 18 February 1880. [St Cuthbert's gravestone] [S.11429]

RICHMOND, ROBERT, a surgeon, son of Matthew Richmond a nurseryman in Edinburgh, died in St Croix, Danish Virgin Islands, on 22 May 1805. [SM.67.885]

RIDDOCH, ALEXANDER, a pilot in Leith, testament, 1824, Comm. Edinburgh. [NRS.CC8.8.150.35]

RIDLEY, DAVID, in New Brunswick, heir to his grand-uncle James Ridley, sr., a merchant in Leith, who died in 1804. [NRS.S/H]

RIGGS, HUGH, in Cowfeeder Row, Edinburgh, a victim of theft in 1849. [NRS.AD14.49.118]

RITCHIE, CHRISTIAN, relict of Lieutenant John Aire, residing in Springfield, Leith Walk, Edinburgh, an inventory, 21 November 1847. [NRS]

RITCHIE, EUPHAN, born 1772 in Edinburgh, was naturalised in Charleston, South Carolina, on 26 June 1832. [NARA.M1183.1]

RITCHIE, JAMES, a shipmaster in Leith, testament, 1803, Comm. Edinburgh. [NRS.CC8.8.134.291]

RITCHIE, J., a clock and watchmaker, 29 Leith Street, Edinburgh, 1849. [POD]

RITCHIE, JOHN, born 1754, a slater and builder, died in November 1805, husband of Janet Sibbald, born 1760, died in September 1824. [Greyfriars gravestone]

RITCHIE, JOHN, son of John Ritchie and his wife Margaret Irvine in the Canongait, died in Nashville, Tennessee, in August 1864. [East Preston Street gravestone, Edinburgh]

RITCHIE, NICOL, son of George Ritchie a coachman, was apprenticed to Francis Howden, a locksmith in Edinburgh, for seven years, on 9 January 1800. [ERA]

RITCHIE, THOMAS, a shipmaster in Leith, testament, 1820, Comm. Edinburgh. [NRS.CC8.8.146.186]

RITCHIE, WILLIAM, was apprenticed to John Cheyne, a surgeon in Leith, for five years, on 13 September 1798. [ERA]

ROBERTS, MERCER, son of Edward Roberts a saddler in Williamsburgh, Virginia, was apprenticed to Baillie Blinshall a saddler in Edinburgh, for seven years, on 15 October 1778. [ERA]

ROBERTSON, ADAM SWANSTON, son of James Robertson in Edinburgh, a farmer in Port Phillip, Victoria, Australia, by 1845. [NRS.S/H]

ROBERTSON, ALEXANDER, born 1775 in Edinburgh, emigrated to New Brunswick in 1798, married Margaret Stuart in St John, NB, in 1804, died in 1842. [BAF] [BLG]

ROBERTSON, ALEXANDER, an elder of South Leith parish on 1 October 1843. [SLR]

ROBERTSON, DAVID, a baker and innkeeper in St Andrew Street, Leith, versus John Cook, a gardener on Leith Walk, a Process of Scandal in 1795. [NRS.CC8.6.970]

ROBERTSON, DONALD, born 1843 in Canonmills, Edinburgh, son of John Robertson, died in Jersey City, New Jersey, on 28 March 1872. [S.8962]

ROBERTSON, DUNCAN, from Carronvale and Friendship in St Elizabeth, Jamaica, died in Edinburgh on 12 February 1824. [DPCA]

ROBERTSON, ELIZABETH, widow of M. Sully in Richmond, Virginia, heir to her sister Margaret Robertson, also, to her husband James. Gilchrist an architect in Edinburgh, 1827. [NRS.S/H]

ROBERTSON, GEORGE, formerly a merchant in Leith, died in Monte Video, Uruguay, on 6 August 1807. [SM.69.958]

ROBERTSON, J. THOMAS, an elder of South Leith parish on 1 October 1843. [SLR]

ROBERTSON, JAMES, MD, Fellow of the Royal College of Physicians of Edinburgh, formerly a surgeon in the Naval Hospital in Barbados, died in Jamaica on 11 December 1811. [SM.74.238]

ROBERTSON, JAMES, born 1777 in Edinburgh, a confectioner, with his wife Margaret, born 1781 in Edinburgh, and children, Margaret born 1804, Jean born 1813, James born 1816, and John born 1819, emigrated via Greenock to America before 1819, were naturalised in New York on 31 May 1823. [NY Court of Common Pleas Records]

ROBERTSON, JAMES, born 1798, 'for 41 years the robe-keeper to the Faculty of Advocates', died on 17 December 1868, husband of Helen Graham, born 1796, died on 30 June 1838. [St Cuthbert's gravestone]

ROBERTSON, JAMES, from Edinburgh, emigrated with his wife Margaret MacGregor, and family, via Greenock aboard the brig Niagara, Captain Hamilton, bound for Montreal, Quebec, in 1825, settled in McNab, Bathurst, Upper Canada. [SG]

ROBERTSON, JAMES, born 10 January 1833 in Edinburgh, son of John Robertson, a book distributor in New York, died in London on 30 April 1920. [ANY]

ROBERTSON, JAMES, a merchant from Edinburgh, died in Rondeboek, Cape of Good Hope, South Africa, on 16 January 1849. [SG.1811]

ROBERTSON, or CROOM, JANET, in Boston, USA, a sasine, 26 May 1854. [NRS.RS.Edinburgh.65.117]

ROBERTSON, JOHN, born 1787 in Edinburgh, a carpenter who died in Savanna, Georgia. On 6 September 1809. [Savanna Death Register]

ROBERTSON, JOHN, a wharfinger in Kingston, Jamaica, eldest son of John Robertson in Canongaithead, Edinburgh, died in Port Royal, Jamaica, on 3 April 1807. [SM.69.957]

ROBERTSON, JOHN, in Canada, heir to David Robertson, chamberlain in Edinburgh, who died on 24 October 1871. [NRS.S/H]

ROBERTSON, JOHN, born 1854 in Edinburgh, died in New York on 5 June 1885. [S.13077]

ROBERTSON, JOHN STUART, born 1855, son of Dr Joseph Robertson of HM Register House in Edinburgh, died in Louisville, Kentucky, on 3 October 1884. [S.12906]

ROBERTSON, PAMELA, wife of C. L. Robertson in America, heir of Jane Robertson, widow of J. Livingstone a merchant on South Bridge, Edinburgh, 1860. [NRS.S/H]

ROBERTSON, PETER, youngest son of John Robertson sr., a baker in Edinburgh, died in Valparaiso, Chile, on 18 May 1876. [S.10285]

ROBERTSON, ROBERT, born on 6 April 1740 in Edinburgh, was admitted as a Freeman of New York on 7 February 1769, a merchant there, died on 6 November 1805, buried in Trinity Churchyard, N.Y. [ANY]

ROBERTSON, ROBERT, son of George Robertson a journeyman tailor, was apprenticed to Thomas Chalmers a locksmith in Edinburgh, for six years on 2 May 1800. [ERA]

ROBERTSON, ROBERT, born 1851, youngest son of Thomas Robertson of 11 Grange Road, Edinburgh, died in Portage la Prairie, Manitoba, on 3 March 1884. [EC.31032]

ROBISON, WILLIAM, was found guilty of forgery in Edinburgh and sentenced to transportation to the colonies for fourteen years, in February 1790. [AJ.2198]

RODGERS, JOHN, a Customs officer in Leith, died 1791, husband of Catherine Paterson, born in 1740, died on 28 August 1818. [Greyfriars gravestone]

ROGERS, JOHN, in St Petersburg, Russia, grand-nephew of Thomas Rogers, a merchant in Edinburgh, 1841. [NRS.S/H]

ROLAND, GEORGE, a teacher of fencing at the Royal Academy, 86 South Bridge, Edinburgh, 1849. [POD]

ROLLO, DAVID, son of William Rollo in the Canongate, was apprenticed to Innes and Wallace, gunsmiths in Edinburgh, for six years on 31 January 1799. [ERA]

ROMANES, GEORGE JOHN, born 20 May 1848, in Elmsley, Canada, son of Reverend George Romanes, [1805-1871], and his wife Isabella Cair, [1810-1883], died in Oxford, England, on 23 May 1894. [Greyfriars gravestone, Edinburgh]

ROMANES, GEORGINA, bornin October 1842, in Elmsley, Canada, son of Reverend George Romanes, [1805-1871], and his wife Isabella Cair, [1810-1883], died in London, England, on 1 April 1878. [Greyfriars gravestone, Edinburgh]

ROMANES, ROBERT ROSE, born in November 1838, in Elmsley, Canada, son of Reverend George Romanes, [1805-1871], and his wife Isabella Cair, [1810-1883], died in Kingston, Canada, on 9 March 1849. [Greyfriers gravestone, Edinburgh]

RONALD, JOHN, son of William Ronald a gardener near Leith, was apprenticed to Charles Robertson, a painter in Edinburgh, for six years on 20 August 1795. [ERA]

RONALDSON, JAMES, born 1768, in Gorgie, Edinburgh, son of William Ronaldson, [1738-1817], and his wife Marion Cleghorn, [1734-1825], a printer or typefounder, who settled in Philadelphia, Pennsylvania, in 1794, a sasine, 20 June 1828, died in Philadelphia on 29 March 1841.
[NRS.RS.Edinburgh,32.78][AP][OEC.28.45][NRS.RD5.367.338]

RONALDSON, JANET, daughter of William Robertson of Gorgie, [1737-1817], and his wife Marion Cleghorn, [1734-1825], settled in Philadelphia, Pennsylvania, died on 16 October 1834, testament, 1835. [NRS.SC70.1.53][Colinton gravestone]

RONALDSON, JOHN, second son of Archibald Ronaldson in Leith, died in Philadelphia, Pennsylvania, on 2 January 1842. [EEC.20323]

RONALDSON, RICHARD, born 1772, in Gorgie, Edinburgh, son of William Ronaldson, [1738-1817], a baker burgess, and his wife Marion Cleghorn, [1734-1825], a jeweller who settled in Philadelphia, Pennsylvania, before 1823, died in Philadelphia on 16 July 1863. [OEC.28.45][S.2517][Colinton gravestone]

RONALDSON, WILLIAM, born 1805 in Leith, eldest son of Archibald Ronaldson, died on 7 September 1834, as did his wife Helen born 1805, and their children Ellen born 1828, Arthur Weatherly born 1830, Jane Marion born 1832, and Robert born 1827, died when the boiler of the Lady of the Lake, a steam packet, burst near Quebec. [AJ.4529]

RONALDSON, WILLIAM, son of William Robertson, [1739-1817], and his wife Marion Cleghorn, [1734-1825], in Colinton, died at Martha Bay, Jamaica, before 1840. [Colinton gravestone]

RONALDSON, Miss, a drawing teacher, 15 Chapel Street, Edinburgh, 1849. [POD]

ROSA, EDWARD, chiropodist, 35 Castle Street, Edinburgh, 1849. [POD]

ROSE, ELIZABETH MUNRO, daughter of George Munro in Grenada, married Robert Rowley, a Captain of the Royal Navy, in Edinburgh, on 30 September 1822. [DPCA.1054]

ROSE, HARRIET, daughter of James Rose, the Deputy Clerk of Session in Edinburgh, died in Demerara on 16 September 1822. [BM.12.803]

ROSE, JOHN EXLEY, eldest son of Neilson Rose of the Carron Company in Leith, died in Santarem, Brazil, on 15 May 1872. [S.9032]

ROSE, MARY, eldest daughter of James Rose the Deputy Clerk of Session, married Colin Campbell from Demerara, in Edinburgh on 10 July 1821. [EA.6032.183]

ROSE, HUGH, a Lieutenant Colonel in Portuguese Service, married Catharine Waddell, eldest daughter of James Waddell of Kingston, Jamaica, in Edinburgh on 23 December 1821. [DPCA.1066]; parents of a daughter Mary, who died in Somerset Park, Liguena, St Andrew, Jamaica, on 22 April 1826, [EA.6538.448], and another daughter born in Kingston, Jamaica, on 6 June 1826. [EA]

ROSS, ALEXANDER, elder of South Leith parish in 1825. [SLR]; a writer in Leith, a petitioner in 1828. [SLR]

ROSS, D. W., born 1778, late Captain of the 31st Regiment of Foot, died in Edinburgh on 4 October 1851; husband of Ann Martin, born 1791, died 23 February 1863. [St Cuthbert's gravestone, Edinburgh]

ROSS, WILLIAM, son of Daniel Ross a porter, was apprenticed to Mark and Charles Kerr, His Majesty's Printers for Scotland, for seven years, on 2 December 1790. [ERA]

ROSS, WILLIAM, of Skeldon, born 1788, died in Berbice on 19 February 1840. [Greyfriars gravestone]

ROSS, WILLIAM, formerly in Berbice, later in Edinburgh, a sasine in 1849. [NRS.RS38.GR2471/131]

ROUGHHEAD, WILLIAM, jr., a hosier and glover, 69 George Street, Edinburgh, in 1849. [POD]

ROWAND, ALEXANDER, MD in Montreal, married Margaret Kincaid, daughter of the late Thomas Kincaid a merchant in Leith, in Edinburgh on 25 January 1844. [GM.ns.21.309]

ROWE, ROBERT, a cabinetmaker in New York, son and heir of Margaret Youngson, wife of Robert Rowe, a porter in Edinburgh, in 1818. [NRS.S/H]

ROY, JAMES, a lace dealer, 24 North Bridge, Edinburgh, in 1849. [POD]

RUDDIMAN, JOHN, a cutler and surgical instrument maker, 5 Hanover Street, Edinburgh, 1849. [POD]

RUDDIMAN, WALTER, son of Thomas Ruddiman a printer in Edinburgh, a midshipman aboard HMS Venus, a frigate, died in the West Indies on 10 May 1813. [SM.75.478]

RUNCIMAN, Reverend DAVID, and his wife Margaret Aitchison in Edinburgh, parents of ROBERT INGLIS RUNCIMAN, born 9 April 1848, a merchant in Buenos Ayres, Argentina, he married Mary Spring, daughter of Andrew Spring from Portland, Maine, in Buenos Ayres on 24 April 1876, parents of a son born there on 23 January 1877. [F.3.435] [EC.28576] [S.10228]; Also, ELIZABETH ISABELLA RUNCIMAN, born in Edinburgh on 14 December 1855, who married George O'Connell, and died in Venado, Tuerto, Argentina, on 4 August 1918. [F.3.435]; asl, parents of JOHN AITCHISON RUNCIMAN, born in Edinburgh on 6 June 1842, a banker in Pietermaritzburg, South Africa, who died in 1902. [F.3.435]

RUSSELL, ARCHIBALD, third son of James Russell, a Professor of Clinical Surgery at Edinburgh University, died at 21 West 10th Street, New York, on 17 April 1871. [S.8662]

RUSSELL, JAMES, son of David Russell a tailor in Simon's Square, Edinburgh, was apprenticed to Joh Dewar a shoemaker in Edinburgh, for seven years on 2 April 1795. [ERA]

RUSSELL, ROBERT, a boy from George Watson's Hospital, was apprenticed to James Thomson, a brewer in Edinburgh, for five years on 29 November 1799. [ERA]

RUSSELL, ROBERT, a wright from Edinburgh, later in New York by 1819. [NRS.CS17.1.39/491]

RUSSELL, ROBERT, a leather dresser and wool merchant in Canonmills, Edinburgh, in 1849. [POD]

RUTHERFORD, A., born 1818, from Edinburgh, died at 194 George Street, Toronto, Ontario, on 6 April 1874. [EC.27946]

RUTHERFORD, CHRISTIAN, youngest daughter of Dr John Rutherford the Professor of Materia Medico at Edinburgh University, died in Edinburgh on 18 November 1819. [SM.85]

RUTHERFORD, Dr DANIEL, the Professor of Botany at Edinburgh University, died on 15 December 1819. [SM.85]

RUTHVEN, JAMES, born 1776 in Edinburgh, died on the SS Louisiana between New Orleans, Louisiana, and Galveston, Texas, in 1853. [EEC.33432]

RUTHVEN, JAMES, born 1783 in Edinburgh, son of John Ruthven and his wife Elizabeth Irvine, a horner in Bridgeport, Connecticut, and in New York, died there on 25 November 1855. [ANY]; his widow Jane, from Edinburgh, died at 144 West 23rd Street, N.Y., in 1874. [S9592]

RUTHVEN, JOHN, a printing and copying press maker, 23 New Street, Edinburgh, 1849. [POD] Samuel John Collymore, from Barbados, in Edinburgh on 23 August 181. [SM.73.716]

RYMER, JESSY, youngest daughter of Dr Rymer, married Dr

SAMPSON, JOHN, a skipper in Leith, son-in-law of baillie Thomas Wardlaw of Dunfermline, Fife, was admitted as a burgess of Dunfermline on 26 May 1796. [DM]

SAMUELS, PAUL STEVENS, born 1774, an MD in Edinburgh later in Negril Spots, Jamaica, died on 18 November 1850. [Dean gravestone]

SANDEMAN, D., wool dealer, 9 Greenside Street, Edinburgh, 1849. [POD]

SANDERSON, CHARLES, from Edinburgh, father of James Sanderson, an infant, also Maria Sanderson, an infant, who died at 548 Hudson Street, New York, on 25 May 1869 and on 2 June 1869. [S.8082]

SANDERSON, PATRICK, born 1759, a banker who died in 1830, husband of Helen Christie, born 1772, died in 1849. [St John's gravestone, Edinburgh]

SANDERSON, PATRICK, and his wife Mary McQueen in Edinburgh, parents of Patrick Sanderson a Captain in the Service of the East India Company, 1833. [NRS.S/H]

SANDFORD, Mrs ANN, born 1 April 1821 in Edinburgh, wife of Thomas Sandford, died in Durham, North Carolina, on 1 November 1887. [Cross Creek gravestone, N.C.]

SANDFORD, DANIEL KEYR, son of Reverend Daniel Sandford and his wife Helen Frances ....., was born on 3 February 1798 and baptised in the church of St John the Evangelist in Edinburgh, on 26 February 1798. [NRS.CH12.3.26.3]

SANDS, WILLIAM JOHN, in Edinburgh, in the Service of the East India Company, died on 10 January 1837, inventory 1837. [NRS]

SAUNDERS, JOHN, son of James Saunders a Writer to the Signet, was apprenticed to James Hall a merchant in Leith, for five years, on 23 November 1797. [ERA]

SAUNDERS, JOHN, a wright in Mitchell Street, Leith, the Convenor of the Incorporated Trades of Leith, 1849. [SLR]

SCALES, ANDREW, jr., a merchant in Leith, trading with Demerara in 1807-1808. [NRS.CS96.783]

SCALES, ANDREW, an elder of South Leith parish on 1 October 1843. [SLR]

SCARTH, JAMES, deacon of South Leith parish in 1825. [SLR]; a merchant in Leith, a petitioner in 1828; an elder on 1 October 1843. [SLR]

SCHETKY, GEORGE, born June 1776 in Edinburgh, son of J.G. S. Schetky and his wife Maria Reinagle, married Elizabeth Paterson, daughter of Stephen Paterson, a merchant in Philadelphia, Pennsylvania, there on 1 January 1823. [SM.86.518; SM.91.518]

SCOTLAND, T., navigation teacher, 40 Bridge Street, Leith,1849. [POD]

SCOTT, ADAM BISSET, a tailor in Leith, who died on 15 November 1872, father of Donald Scott, a farmer in Kiata, Victoria, Australia. [NRS.S/H]

SCOTT, ARCHIBALD, born 1778, a solicitor and a procurator fiscal, died on 7 December 1848, husband of Catharine Gray, born 1780, died on 3 December 1857. [Greyfriars gravestone]

SCOTT, CHARLOTTE SOPHIA, daughter of Walter Scott, an advocate, and his wife Margaret Charlotte ....., was born on 24 October 1799, and baptised in the church of St John the Evangelist in Edinburgh, on 15 November 1799. [NRS.CH12.3.26.7]

SCOTT, DAVID, son of Alexander Scott a merchant in Edinburgh, died in the West Indies on 26 June 1787. [SM.49.466]

SCOTT, ELIZA, wife of James Alexander from Edinburgh, died in Toronto, Ontario, on 29 December 1859. [W.21.2163]

SCOTT, ELIZABETH, from Edinburgh, later in America, a sasine 1831. [NRS.RS.Edinburgh.38.125]

SCOTT, GEORGE ROBERTSON, born 3 May 1793, son of George Robertson Scott, an advocate, and his wife Isabella Pattison, a Captain of Artillery in the Bengal Army, India, died on 19 August 1854. [BA]

SCOTT, HUGH, of Gala, Selkirkshire, a letter to the Duke of Buccleuch, from Niagara, Canada, in 1791. [NRS.GD224.box31.19.2.6]

SCOTT, ISAAC, postmaster, Braehouse, Edinburgh, 1849. [POD]

SCOTT, JAMES CORSE, born 2 June 1810 in Edinburgh, son of John Corse Scott and his wife Catherine ....., to India in 1826, Major General of the Bengal Army, in India, died in Edinburgh on 7 March 1890. [BA]

SCOTT, JOHN, [1790-1857], in Fountainbridge, Edinburgh, husband of Margaret Henry. [St Cuthbert's gravestone]

SCOTT, JOHN, a merchant and a tenant in the Bush, Leith, in 1811. [LD]

SCOTT, KEZIA, from Edinburgh, later in America, a sasine, 15 June 1831. [NRS.RS.Edinburgh.38.125]

SCOTT, MATTHEW, born 1845, son of Andrew Scott, [1803-1883], and his wife Margaret Henderson, [1814-1894], died in Corona, Australia, on 4 June 1908. [Colinton gravestone]

SCOTT, MICHAEL, born 30 October 1789 in Edinburgh, a writer and a merchant in Jamaica from 1806 and 1822, died in Glasgow on 6 November 1835. [Glasgow Necropolis gravestone]

SCOTT, ROBERT, born on 2 October 1745 in Edinburgh, emigrated to Virginia, a mathematician and engraver, died in Philadelphia, Pennsylvania, on 3 November 1823, buried in the Friends Burial Ground. [AP]

SCOTT, THOMAS BONNAR, born 1841, son of Alexander Scott a farmer in Craiglockhart, a planter in Fiji, died 30 June 1882. [Colinton gravestone]

SCOTT, WILLIAM HENRY, son of Alexander Scott a merchant in Edinburgh, a merchant on St Eustatia, Dutch West Indies, died in Antigua on 12 May 1789. [SM.51.361]

SCOTT, WILLIAM, from Naples, Italy, married Janette Cormack, daughter of Alexander Cormack in St John, Newfoundland, in Edinburgh in May 1824. [S.458.344]

SCOTT, WILLIAM, a pewterer, 108 West Bow, Edinburgh, 1849. [POD]

SCOUGALL, G., a corn merchant, 15 Quality Street, Edinburgh, 1849. [POD]

SCOUGALL, RICHARD, from Leith, died at the house of his daughter Mrs Liston in Montreal, Quebec, on 11 September 1841. [AJ.4892] [EEC.20269]

SCRYMGEOUR, JAMES, from Edinburgh, died in New York on 12 May 1851. [EEC.22129]

SCRYMGEOUR, JOHN, was baptised in Edinburgh on 30 November 1746, son of David Scrymgeour of Birkhill and his wife Katherine Wedderburn, a Captain of the Bengal Army, he died in Mysore, India, on 3 March 1791. [BA]

SCRYMGEOUR, WILLIAM, son of John Scrymgeour a wright, was apprenticed to Thomas Chalmers, a locksmith in Edinburgh, for seven years, on 11 June 1795. [ERA]

SELKRIG, ROBERT, from Demerara, died in Edinburgh on 5 March 1823. [SM.111.520]

SETON HENRY, veterinary surgeon, 129 Rose Street Lane, Edinburgh, 1849. [POD]

SHAND, JAMES, son of John Shand a shoemaker, was apprenticed to Andrew Hay, a shoemaker in Edinburgh, for six years on 6 February 1800. [ERA]

SHANKLIE, PETER, late of Leith Walk Nursery, Edinburgh, died on the Estancia de San Jorge, Argentina, in 1853. [S.26.10.1853]

SHAW, JAMES, a boatbuilder in 15 St Anthony Place, Edinburgh, in 1849. [POD]

SHEARER, ALEXANDER, born 1782, a builder in Edinburgh, died on 15 November 1819. [SM.85]

SHEARER, THOMAS, from Edinburgh, in New York by 1812. [NRS.CS17.1.31/573; 7/265]; probate 1852, PCC. [TNA]

SHEPPARD, JOHN, born 1794, a painter, died 1857, and his wife Alison Darey, born 1800, died 1846, parents of John Sheppard, born 1833, who died at his estancia near Monte Video, Uruguay, on 1 November 1868. [St Cuthbert's gravestone] [S.8085]

SHERIFF, ARTHUR MCEWEN, born 15 April 1822 in Edinburgh, son of Reverend Thomas Sheriff and his wife Janet McEwen, a minister in Australia from 1849, died in New South Wales on 8 November 1864. [F.1.319]

SHIELD, JAMES ARRAN, born 1 January 1844, son of George Shield, [1806-1898], and his wife Mary Dickson, [1816-1898], died in Buffalo, New York on 5 May 1886. [Dean gravestone, Edinburgh]

SHIRREFF, ADAM DIXON, born 1784 in Leith, died in Chatham, New Brunswick, on 21 January 1839. [St Andrews Standard, 16.2.1839]

SHIRREFF, JOHN, from Leith, died at Chaffrey Mills, Upper Canada, on 23 September 1828. [BM.25.268]

SHIRREFF, ROBERT, in Fitzroy, Canada West, son and heir of Charles Shirreff, a merchant from Leith, later in Fitzroy, in 1849. [NRS.S/H]

SHORT, AGNES, widow of Robert Gow in Edinburgh, heir to her uncle Robert Gow, a planter in Jamaica, in 1854. [NRS.S/H]

SHORT, ROBERT, a mariner in Leith, inventory, 1809, Comm. Edinburgh. [NRS.SC70.1.1.609]

SHORT, WILLIAM, a vintner and a tenant in the Bush, Leith, in 1811. [LD]

SIBBALD, J., an ironmonger, 64 George Street, Edinburgh, in 1849. [POD]

SIBBALD, LESLEY, a shipmaster in Leith, inventory, 1811, Comm. Edinburgh. [NRS.SC70.1.3.330]

SIEVEWRIGHT, ANDREW GRAHAM, born 1802, third son of ..... Mr Sievewright, of Arniston Place, Edinburgh, died on Hallhead Estate, Jamaica, on 13 September 1821. [DPCA][BM.11.133]

SIM, HENRY, son of George Sim a tobacconist in Leith, died in Jamaica in 1813. [EA.5216.13]

SIMPSON, ALEXANDER, born 1780, a merchant from West Church parish in Edinburgh, emigrated to New York aboard the George of New York on 12 August 1807. [NRS.PC1.3790]

SIMSON, ALEXANDER, an elder of South Leith parish on 1 October 1843. [SLR]

SIMSON, Dr ANDREW, in Edinburgh, in the Service of the East India Company, died 30 August 1843, inventory 1844. [NRS]

SIMPSON, CHARLES, son of Alexander Simpson a shoemaker in the Canongait, was apprenticed to Anthony Wilkieson, a gunsmith in Edinburgh, for seven years, in 1798. [ERA]

SIMPSON, EDWARD, in Edinburgh, father of Colonel JOHN Simpson in the Service of the East India Company, 1835. [NRS.S/H]

SIMPSON, HOUSTON, master of the Cumberland of Leith which foundered on passage from Jamaica on 22 August 1806, he was rescued but died in Baltimore, Maryland, on 24 September 1806. [SM.69.77]

SIMPSON, JOHN, from Edinburgh, a theological student in the 1820s, later a minister in Port Maria, Jamaica. [UPC]

SIMPSON, JOHN, in Forth Street, Edinburgh, a Colonel in the Service of the East India Company, died on 20 June 1836, an inventory 1836. [NRS]

SIMSON, JOHN, an elder of South Leith parish on 1 October 1843. [SLR]

SINCLAIR, FINLAY, a farmer in Canada, brother and heir of Daniel Sinclair in Edinburgh, in 1857. [NRS.S/H]

SINCLAIR, JANE, eldest daughter of John Sinclair in North Leith, married James Downie an engineer, in Valparaiso, Chile, on 6 August 1862. [S.2276]

SINCLAIR, J., a tartan manufacturer, 79 South Bridge, Edinburgh, in 1849. [POD]

SINCLAIR, MALCOLM, born 1766, formerly a merchant in Leith, died in Gothenburg, Sweden, on 5 April 1854. [W.xv.1537]

SINCLAIR, THOMAS, from Leith, married Jessie Glass Gow, daughter of James Gow in Edinburgh, in Valparaiso, Chile, on 25 November 1870. [S.8583]; parents of a son born in Valparaiso on 25 September 1871. [S.8831]

SINCLAIR and WILLIAMSON, merchants in Leith, 1796. [NRS.CS97.112.62]

SINTON, W., a slater, 11 St Leonard's Lane, Edinburgh, 1849. [POD]

SKAE, D. E., a medical practitioner, Lunatic Asylum, Edinburgh, 1849. [POD]

SKEAF, or GORDON, MARY, wife of Andrew Gordon, a saddler from Ballater, Aberdeenshire, later in Canada, grand-daughter and heir of Joseph Skeaf, a quill manufacturer in Edinburgh, who died on 4 March 1833. [NRS.S/H]

SKIRVEN, GEORGE, a shipmaster in Leith, testament, 1804, Comm. Edinburgh. [NRS]

SLIGHT, JAMES, an engineer, 34 Leith Walk, Edinburgh, 1849. [POD]

SLIMMON, Mrs, trimming warehouse, 55 Tolbooth Wynd, Leith, 1849. [POD]

SMALL, A., a provision merchant, 19 Charles Street, Edinburgh, 1849. [POD]

SMALL, MARGARET, born 1844, wife of William Keith a law accountant from Edinburgh, died in New York on 3 November 1877. [S.10717]

SMART, CHARLES MORTON, born 1845, youngest son of Dr Smart, died in Chicago, Illinois, on 29 August 1882, was buried in Graceland Cemetery there. [South Leith gravestone]

SMART, WILLIAM, a merchant in Edinburgh, father of John Smart, born 1860, died in Duluth, Minnesota, on 28 November 1884. [S.12928]

SMELLIE, ALEXANDER, printer, 2 Thistle Street, Edinburgh, 1849. [POD]

SMELLIE, THOMAS, born 1810, youngest son of Robert Smellie a grocer in Tobago Street, Edinburgh, died in New York on 28 December 1868. [S.7977]

SMIBERT, A., smith, 5 St Andrew Street, Leith, 1849. [POD]

SMILES, T., brewer, 46 Tolbooth Wynd, Leith, 1849. [POD]

SMITH, Mrs AGNES, born 1759 in Edinburgh, relict of John Smith a merchant, died on 11 February 1834. [Old Scots gravestone, South Carolina]

SMITH, BERNARD, from Leith, later in New York in 1809. [NRS.CS17.1.29/218]

SMITH, C. H. J., a landscape and garden architect, 41 Queen Street, Edinburgh, in 1849. [POD]

SMITH, DAVID, a tailor in Rose Street, Edinburgh, versus Sophia McLean, were married in 1805, and divorced in 1822, a Process of Divorce. [NRS.CC8.5.41]

SMITH, JOHN, master of the Edward of Leith from Leith to Pennsylvania and Virginia in 1822, and to Philadelphia in 1823. [EEC.17260] [LCL.X.932]

SMITH, JOHN BAIRD, youngest son of Adam Smith in Stockbridge, Edinburgh, died on passage from Jamaica to America in February 1823. [S.382.576]

SMITH, JOHN DUNCAN, in Rochester, New York, brother and heir of Jessie Smith in Edinburgh, who died on 28 June 1863. [NRS.S/H]

SMITH, GEORGE, a skipper in Leith, husband of Grizel Gilbert, in 1798. [NRS.S/H]

SMITH, JAMES, a tailor in Edinburgh, was admitted as a burgess and guilds-brother of Dunfermline on 26 September 1791. [DM]

SMITH, JAMES, in Harper's Land, South Leith, was granted a beggar's badge on 18 February 1794. [SLR]

SMITH, JAMES, and Company, wholesale merchants, ship-owners and agents, tenants in the Bush, Leith, in 1811. [LD]

SMITH, JOHN, a shipmaster in Leith, testament, 1820, Comm. Edinburgh. [NRS]

SMITH, JOHN, late in the Service of the East India Company, died in Edinburgh on 17 June 1826, inventory 1827. [NRS]

SMITH, JOHN P., son of James Smith in George Street, Edinburgh, died in Jackson, Mississippi, in 1853. [S.22.10.1853]

SMITH, PETER, born 1806, died in Bathurst, New South Wales, Australia, on 24 September 1886. [St Cuthbert's gravestone, Edinburgh]

SMITH, ROBERT, a tailor in Leith, husband of Mary Wilson, whose brother James Wilson was at the College of William and Mary in Virginia, 1792. [NRS.S/H]

SMITH, ROBERT A., born 1836 in Edinburgh, Colonel of the 10th Mississippi Regiment of the Confederate States Army, was killed at the Battle of Mumfordville, Kentucky, on 14 September 1862. [Dean gravestone, Edinburgh]

SMITH, WILLIAM, a tinplate worker in Edinburgh, was admitted as a burgess and guilds-brother of Dunfermline, Fife, on 22 March 1794. [DM]

SMITH, WILLIAM, married Jessie May, daughter of William May a surgeon in New York, in Edinburgh on 21 December 1820. [S.211.391]

SMITH, WILLIAM EBENEZER, an engineer in Aurora, Illinois, brother and heir of Henry Smith, a photographic artist in Edinburgh, who died on 8 February 1868. [NRS.S/H]

SMITH, WILLIAM GRIFFITH, born 1842, from Edinburgh, died in New York on 15 December 1898. [S.17326]

SNODGRASS, J., an apothecary in 238 Canongate, Edinburgh, 1849. [POD]

SOFELY, THOMAS, born 1771, a mason in East Duddingston, died on 14 August 1816, father of Thomas Sofely a wright. [Duddingston gravestone]

SOMERVILLE, AGNES, widow of George Noble, late in Jamaica, died on 20 August 1804. [St Cuthbert's gravestone, Edinburgh]

SOMERVILLE, ALEXANDER, a merchant in Leith, versus David Stewart, a merchant in Leith, in Upper India 1798. [NRS.CS97.16.84]

SOMERVILLE, ANDREW, of the Edinburgh Slaughterhouse, father of Robert Bruce Somerville, born 1861, died in Madras, India, on 7 September 1884. [S.12864]

SOMMERVAIL, JEAN, in Muckle's Close, South Leith, was granted a beggar's badge on 18 February 1794. [SLR]

SOUTAR, J. J., a die and stamp cutter, 31 North Bridge, Edinburgh, 1849. [POD]

SPANKIE, GEORGE, a merchant, died on 13 May 1815, husband of Mary Smith, died on 1 January 1823. [Greyfriars gravestone]

SPAVEN, Mrs, a straw and Leghorn hat maker, 31 Greenside Street, Edinburgh, 1849. [POD]

SPEAR, JOSEPH, born in 1754, a Captain of the Royal Navy, died in 1826. [St John's gravestone, Edinburgh]

SPENCE, JOHN, born 1820 in Leith, son of Alexander Spence a banker, a Lieutenant of the 42 Bengal Light Infantry, who was killed at the Battle of Mookdee, Upper India, on 18 December 1845. [SLR]

SPENCE, ROBERT, eldest son of .... Spence a jeweller in Edinburgh, died in Pennant Valley, Jamaica, on 21 May 1812. [SM.74.727]

SPENCE, THOMAS, a surgeon, son of James Spence a perfumer in Edinburgh, died in Jamaica in January 1803. [EA.4113.03]

SPINKS, CHARLES, turner, 89 St Andrew Street, Leith, 1849. [POD]

SPITTALL, JAMES, son of James Spittall a skipper in Leith, was apprenticed to William Gibson, a merchant in Edinburgh, for six years, in 1796. [ERA]

STABLES, JOHN, a shipmaster in Leith, testament, 1816, Comm. Edinburgh. [NRS]

STARK, GEORGE, son of George Stark a comb-maker, was apprenticed to Alexander Laidlaw a white iron smith in Edinburgh, for six years on 27 April 1797. [ERA]

STARK, JOHN C., born 1812, son of …. Stark and his wife Emma Brown, died in Philadelphia, Pennsylvania, on 29 December 1838. [St Cuthbert's gravestone, Edinburgh]

STEDMAN, HUNTER, born 20 December 1812 in Edinburgh, emigrated to the West Indies in 1839, settled in Philadelphia, Pennsylvania, as a wine merchant, returned to the West Indies in 1890, died in Roseau, Dominica, on 2 September 1900. [AP]

STEDMAN, ROBERT, a soldier of C Company of the Maine Infantry Volunteers, died during the American Civil War, 1861-1865. [Old Calton gravestone]

STEEDMAN, GEORGE, a shipmaster in Leith, testament, 1825, Comm. Edinburgh. [NRS]

STEEL, ALEXANDER, son of Alexander Steel a wright, was apprenticed to Archibald and John McKinlay, merchants in Edinburgh, for six years, on 17 October 1799. [ERA]

STEEL, Miss S., from Edinburgh, married M. Drury from Philadelphia, Pennsylvania, in New York, on 14 May 1823. [EEC.17471][BM.14.1191]

STEILL, ANN, in Tods Hole, South Leith, was granted a beggar's badge on 18 February 1794. [SLR]

STENHOUSE, A., a ship and insurance broker, Wet Docks, Leith, 1849. [POD]

STENHOUSE, REBECCA, daughter of John Stenhouse a baker in Edinburgh, settled in Zante, Greece, by 1841. [NRS.S/H]

STENHOUSE, THOMAS, son of Alexander Stenhouse in Edinburgh, was drowned in the Black River, Poyais, on 12 November 1823. [S.428.103]

STEPHENS, DAVID, a trunk-maker in Edinburgh, father of a son who died in New York in September 1799. [AJ.2718] [NRS.CS233.SEQN.S1.19]

STEUART, JAMES, born 1795, seventh son of David Steuart in Edinburgh, a Lieutenant aboard HMS Hebrus, died on 11 April 1820. [South Park gravestone, Calcutta, India]

STEUART, WILLIAM JOHN, in Binnia Plains, New South Wales, Australia, son and heir of Anne Kennedy or Steuart, in the West Indies, then in Edinburgh, who died on 28 May 1844. [NRS.S/H]

STEVENS, ANDREW, a writer, married Grace B. Campbell, daughter of Colin Campbell in Jamaica, in Edinburgh on 14 February 1806. [DPCA.188]

STEVEN, DAVID, a ham curer, 40 Leith Street, Edinburgh, 1849. [POD]

STEVEN, GEORGE, son of David Steven a mason, was apprenticed to William Auld, a goldsmith in Edinburgh, for seven years, in 1791. [ERA]

STEVEN, WILLIAM, formerly a hat manufacturer in Edinburgh, died in Hamilton, Upper Canada, on 5 March 1845. [EEC.21175]

STEVENSON, HUGH, a merchant in Peru, nephew and heir of Margaret Maule in Edinburgh in 1853. [NRS.S/H]

STEVENSON, JEMIMA ELIZA, youngest daughter of James Stevenson in Leith, married Robert Scarth of Binscarth, at Rideau Cottage, New Edinburgh, Canada West, on 9 April 1855. [W.XVI.1647]

STEVENSON, JAMES, a baker in Gilmerton, versus his wife Janet Fairbairn, a Process of Divorce, in 1819. [NRS.CC8.5.41]

STEVENSON, JOHN, a shoemaker from Edinburgh later in New York, son and heir of James Stevenson in the Canongait, Edinburgh, in 1838. [NRS.S/H]

STEVENSON, ROBERT, son of Allan Stevenson a storekeeper on St Kitts, was apprenticed to Thomas Smith a white ironsmith in Edinburgh for six years on 2 June 1796. [ERA]

STEVENSON, Mrs, from Edinburgh, wife of Henry Stevenson a merchant in New York, died there in 1795. [SM.57.682]

STEWART, ALEXANDER, from Edinburgh, a member of the Scots Charitable Society of Boston, Massachusetts, in 1819. [NEHGS]

STEWART, ANDREW, born 21 February 1799, a painter who was drowned in the Grand River, Upper Canada, on 16 April 1836. [East Preston Street cemetery, Edinburgh]

STEWART, CHARLES, son of James Stewart in Haddington, East Lothian, was apprenticed to Edward Simpson, a barber in Edinburgh, for six years, on 21 June 1792. [ERA]

STEWART, DANIEL, born 1794, a cabinetmaker in Edinburgh, died on 23 September 1864. [St Cuthbert's gravestone, Edinburgh]

STEWART, DAVID, a merchant in Leith, a sasine in 1800. [NRS.RS97.107.6]

STEWART, DAVID, second son of David Stewart of 14 Waterloo Place, Edinburgh, died in Mexico in 1828. [S.885.426]

STEWART, ELIZABETH, daughter of James Stewart in Kingston, Jamaica, died in Edinburgh on 17 August 1798. [EA.3615.119]

STEWART, GEORGE MACKENZIE, a Lieutenant General in the Service of the East India Company, died at 48 Melville Street, Edinburgh, on 23 June 1855, inventory, 1855. [NRS]

STEWART, JAMES HOPE, born 1783, from Edinburgh, emigrated via Oban aboard the Clarendon of Hull bound for Prince Edward Island in August 1808. [TNA.CO226.23]

STEWART, JAMES, born 1804, a coach proprietor in Edinburgh, died on 5 April 1836; husband of Janet Montgomery, born 1799, died 29 January 1859. [St Cuthbert's gravestone]

STEWART, JAMES, a Colonel of the Madras Army, of 6 Melville Crescent, Edinburgh, died 11 February 1864, inventory, 1864. [NRS]

STEWART, Dr JAMES, of Tulloch, married Margaret Walker, third daughter of Hugh Walker in Jamaica, in Edinburgh on 3 August 1840. [AJ.4831]

STEWART, JAMES GAMMELL, an assistant surgeon in the Service of the East India Company, died on 18 April 1858, inventory 1858. [NRS]

STEWART, JOHN, 'late of Jamaica', died on 12 March 1830, husband of Jessie Kemp, [1805-1832]. [St Cuthbert's gravestone]

STEWART, JOHN, of 24 Leith Street, Edinburgh, father of Robert Stewart, a stationer who died in Sydney, New South Wales, Australia, on 16 October 1876. [AJ.6727]

STEWART, JOHN, formerly of 34 Leith Street, Edinburgh, father of a daughter born at Bishop's Avenue, Montreal, Quebec, on 4 August 1875. [EC.28356]

STEWART, KENNETH, from Edinburgh, formerly a Captain of the North Carolina Highlanders, probate July 1815, PCC. [TNA]

STEWART, R., typefounder, 40 Leith Street, Edinburgh, 1849. [POD]

STEWART, ROBERT BRUNTON, son of Mr G. Stewart of Princes Street, Edinburgh, died in Stratford-on-Avon, Canada West, in 1852. [S.22.5.1852]

STEWART, ROBERT, a stationer, son of John Stewart, 24 Leith Street, Edinburgh, died in Sydney, New South Wales, Australia, on 16 October 1876. [AJ.6727]

STEWART, WILLIAM, with three others, from Edinburgh, emigrated via Greenock aboard the Portaferry, Captain Pollock, to Quebec in May 1832. [QM.13.6.1832] [GWS]

STEWART, W., master of the Forest Queen of Leith from Leith with passengers bound for Sydney, New South Wales, Australia, in April 1858. [W.2066]

STOBO, JOHN, a surgeon, married Ann Patnellie, only daughter of George Patnellie, a merchant from Tortula, in Edinburgh, in 1809. [SM.72.77]

STODART, DAVID RIDDLE, born 1832, died on Staten Island, New York, on 14 November 1893. [New Calton gravestone, Edinburgh]

STORIE, JOHN, son of John Storie a merchant in the Grassmarket, Edinburgh, was apprenticed to George Christie, a goldsmith in Edinburgh, for seven years, on 28 April 1796. [ERA]

STOKER, RALPH, a ship owner, 32 Shore, Leith, 1849. [POD]

STOTT, WILLIAM, in Philadelphia, Pennsylvania, brother and heir of Jane Stott, daughter of James Stott a leather merchant in Edinburgh, who did on 31 May 1856. [NRS.S/H]

STRAITON, JOHN, a shipmaster, 4 Hamburg Place, Leith, 1849. [POD]

STRANGE, JAMES, born 1753, died in 1840, husband of Anne ...., born 1767, daughter of Viscount Melville, died in 1852. [St John's gravestone, Edinburgh]

STRATTON, EDWIN W., eldest son of Isaac Stratton in West Swansey, New Hampshire, and son-in-law of Dr W. A. Roberts of 30 Queen Street, Edinburgh, died in Titusville, Pennsylvania, on 30 November 1873. [EC.27832]

STRUTHERS, Dr, a lecturer in practical anatomy, 11 Argyll Square, Edinburgh, in 1849. [POD]

STRUTHERS, ESTHER, daughter of Reverend James Struthers in College Chapel, Edinburgh, married Reverend George Burns, DD, minister of the Scots Kirk in St John, New Brunswick, in St Andrews on 6 August 1827. [BM.22.527]

STRUTHERS, Reverend JAMES, born 31 October 1770, was educated at Glasgow University, minister of the First Relief Church in College Street, Edinburgh, died on 13 July 1807. [Greyfriars gravestone]

STRUTHERS, JAMES, born 1800 in Edinburgh, son of Reverend James Struthers, was educated at the University of St Andrews in 1819, a minister in British Guiana from 1826 to 1857, died in Edinburgh on 4 August 1858. [F.7.675]

STUART, GEORGE ANDREW, in Edinburgh, a surgeon in the Service of the East India Company, died 16 June 1844, an inventory 1844. [NRS]

STUART, HUGH, a writer in Edinburgh, was admitted as a burgess of Dunfermline on 26 September 1791. [DM]

STUART, Dr JOHN GRAHAM, in 54 India Street, Edinburgh, a physician in the Service of the East India Company, died 2 March 1863, an inventory 1863. [NRS]

STUPART, JOHN, a distiller at Yardheads, Edinburgh, 1849. [POD]

SUTHERLAND, JAMES, born 1821, brother of Alexander Sutherland a stationer of 21 George Street, Edinburgh, died in Montreal, Quebec, on 30 April 1874. [EC.27960]

SUTHERLAND, J., a newspaper agent, 12 Calton Street, Edinburgh, 1849. [POD]

SUTHERLAND, JOHN MACKAY, born 1852, died in Ailsa, Paterson, New Jersey, on 14 November 1879. [St Cuthbert's gravestone, Edinburgh]

SUTHERLAND, MARY, widow of Reverend F. Lauder, in Fredericton, USA, niece and heir of Marjory Stuart in Canongait, Edinburgh, in 1795. [NRS.S/H]

SUTHERLAND, WILLIAM, born 1847, died in Ailsa, Paterson, New Jersey, on 28 June 1895. [St Cuthbert's gravestone, Edinburgh]

SWAN, JAMES, a boy from Heriot's Hospital, son of James Swan a wigmaker, was apprenticed to Forrester and Company of the Russia Warehouse, for six years, on 18 August 1791. [ERA]

SWANN, JOHN RUSSELL, born 1821, formerly of the Edinburgh Sawmill in Leith Walk, Edinburgh, died in Dunedin, Otago, New Zealand, on 2 May 1884. [S.12784]

SWANSON, JOHN, a mariner in Leith, testament, 1806, Comm. Edinburgh. [NRS]

SWANSTON, ELIZA, youngest daughter of Dr William Swanston in St Kitts, married John Swanston from Bandon, Ireland, in Edinburgh on 13 December 1824. [S.516.817]

SWANSTON, WILLIAM, late of St Kitts, died 7 July 1820. [Greyfriars gravestone, Edinburgh]

SWINTON, GEORGE, of 4 Athol Crescent, in the Service of the East India Company, of 4 Athol Crescent, Edinburgh, died 17 June 1854, inventory 1854. [NRS]

SYME, ROBERT, in Edinburgh, late in Calcutta, India, died on 2 March 1841, an inventory 1841. [NRS]

TAAP, WILLIAM, a haberdasher, 37 North Bridge, Edinburgh, 1849. [POD]

TAIT, GEORGE, born 1815 in Leith, a merchant in New York, died in New Jersey on 5 August 1886. [ANY]

TANNER, ..., a sailor aboard the Raith of Leith was captured by the French, on the return voyage from Greenland, and imprisoned in Dunkirk, in 1794. [PL.296]

TAWES, JOHN, born 1747, died on 10 July 1832, husband of Christian Bonar, born 1754, died on 23 August 1832. [Grayfriars gravestone]

TAYLOR, DAVID, born 1826, an upholsterer in Edinburgh, died 1855, father of John Taylor, born 1850, a Chartered Accountant, who died in Melbourne, Victoria, Australia, on 27 November 1915. [St Cuthbert's gravestone]

TAYLOR, JAMES YOUNG, born 29 April 1801 in Leith, an entrepreneur, Provost of Leith from 1855 to 1860], died 8 February 1890. [South Leith Church window]

TAYLOR, PETER, a wright in Leith, versus Mary, daughter of the late Ralph Elliot, a shipmaster in Musselburgh, who married on 11 January 1793, a Process of Divorce in April 1796. [NRS.CC8.6.976]

TAYLOR, W., a soap maker, 4 Salamander Street, Edinburgh, 1849. [POD]

TELFER, WILLIAM, a merchant in Leith, father of Christina Maria Telfer, who married Francis Arnold, C.J., M.D., in Montreal, Quebec, on 24 September 1829. [BM.27.133]

TEMPLE, MARGARET, widow of David Brown, a shipbuilder in Leith and Martinique, 1799. [NRS.CS97.105.14]

TEMPLEMAN, Mrs, a midwife, 6 St James Street, Edinburgh, 1849. [POD]

TENCH, CAROLINE MARGARETTA, born 1815, wife of John Laing in Upper Canada, died in Edinburgh on 7 April 1836. [Restalrig gravestone]

THATCHER, Dr, a lecturer in midwifery, Picardy Place, Edinburgh, in 1849. [POD]

THIN, JAMES, bookseller, 14 Infirmary Street, Edinburgh, 1849. [POD]

THIN, Dr ROBERT, born 1794, son of John Thin an architect in Edinburgh, surgeon of the 2nd Ceylon Regiment, died in Columbo, 27 July 1819. [SM.85]

THOMS, WILLIAM, from Edinburgh, father of a daughter born in Yorkville, New York, on 28 February 1852. [FJ.1005]

THOMPSON, ALEXANDER, born 1734, son of James Thompson, [1714-1770], an Excise accountant, and his wife Agnes Smith, [1717-1745], settled in Savannah, Georgia, as Customs Collector, a Loyalist in 1776, settled in Edinburgh by 1788, died there on 25 September 1798. [Canongait gravestone] [TNA.AO12.4.251, etc.][EA.3677/215]

THOMSON, ANDREW, born 1775, from Trinidad, died in Deanhall, Stockbridge, Edinburgh, on 6 March 1820. [BM.7.119]

THOMSON, ANDREW, from Edinburgh, a Captain of the Royal Navy, testament, 1828, Comm. Edinburgh. [NRS]

THOMSON, CHARLES FRIER, born on 9 December 1797, son of John Deas Thomson and his wife Rebecca, was born on 9 December 1797 and baptised in the church of St John the Evangelist, Edinburgh, on 19 January 1798. [NRS.CH12.3.26.3]

THOMSON, DAVID, a carter in Broughton Loan, Edinburgh, was accused of theft and reset in 1815. [NRS.AD14.15.25]

THOMPSON, H. B., in Leith, father of James Thompson, born 1857, an engineer who died in Melbourne, Victoria, Australia, on 8 August 1897. [S.17011]

THOMSON, HENRY, son of James Thomson a schoolmaster in Leith, was apprenticed to William Begbie, a tailor in Edinburgh, for six years, in May 1797. [ERA]

THOMSON, ISABEL, in South Leith, was granted a beggar's badge on 18 February 1794. [SLR]

THOMPSON, J., born 1839, from Edinburgh, died in Buenos Ayres, Argentina, in 1871. [SRP.366]

THOMSON, JAMES, son of Alexander Thomson a brewer, was apprenticed to Alexander Donaldson, a bookseller and printer in Edinburgh, for five years in 1795. [ERA]

THOMSON, JAMES, a merchant from Leith, died in Washington County, Georgia, in February 1807. [SM.69.798][AJ.3114][DPCA.267]

THOMSON, JAMES G. C., born 1840, third son of James Gibson Thomson in Edinburgh, died in Ottawa, Canada, on 1 April 1873. [EC.27628]

THOMSON, JOHN, son of John Deas Thomson and his wife Rebecca, was baptised in the church of St John the Evangelist, Edinburgh, on 6 June 1799. [NRS.CH12.3.26.7]

THOMSON, JOHN, from Leith, a Master of the Royal Navy, testament, 1805, Comm. Edinburgh. [NRS]

THOMSON, JOHN, of Priorletham, born 1754, a merchant in Leith, for 21 years tenant of Easter Duddingston, died 26 September 1820, husband of Margaret Reddie, born 1766, died 12 November 1825. [Duddingston gravestone]

THOMSON, JOHN, in Montreal, Quebec, son and heir of Margaret Robertson, widow of John Thomson, a merchant in Leith, in 1834. [NRS.S/H]

THOMSON, JOHN WALKER, born 1810, son of David Jugurtha Thomson a leather factor in Niddry Street, Edinburgh, died in Clinton, Pennsylvania, on 2 March 1878. [S.10822]

THOMSON, JOHN, in 26 Nelson Street, Edinburgh, father of John Thomson who married Jessie Ramsay, eldest daughter of Gilbert Ramsay from Ayrshire, in Buenos Ayres, Argentina, on 5 March 1862, John died there on 16 April 1871. [S.2147/8684]

THOMSON, MATTHEW, a shoemaker in America, son and heir of David Thomson, a shoemaker in Edinburgh, in 1843. [NRS.S/H]

THOMSON, ROBERT, a clerk in New York, son and heir of John Thomson, a printer in Edinburgh, in 1851. [NRS.S/H]

THOMSON, ROBERT, a merchant in Brighton Street, Edinburgh, father of Robertson Thomson who died in Meadville, Pennsylvania, on 2 April 1870. [S.8345]

THOMSON, THOMAS, son of Alexander Thomson a tobacconist in Edinburgh, an overseer on Plantation Plaisance, East Coast of Dominica, died on 2 May 1824. [DPCA.1146]

THOMSON, THOMAS, elder of South Leith parish in 1825. [SLR]; of the Glassworks in Leith, a petitioner in 1828. [SLR]

THOMSON, THOMAS YULE, born 1847, a baker in 41 Broughton Street, Edinburgh, died in Callao, Peru, on 14 January 1869. [S.8029]

THOMSON, WILLIAM, elder of South Leith parish in 1825. [SLR]; a blockmaker in Leith, a petitioner in 1828; an elder on 1 October 1843. [SLR]

THOMSON, WILLIAM, born 1789, a baker in Edinburgh, died 14 October 1864; husband of Charlotte Parker, born 1791, died 28 March 1864. [St Cuthbert's gravestone, Edinburgh]

THORBURN, Reverend David, minister of the Second Charge in Leith until 1843 when he entered the Free Church of Scotland. [SLR]

TIBBETS, WILLIAM, son of Thomas Tibbets a hatmaker, was apprenticed to John Armour and Company, merchants in Edinburgh, for five years, on 1 March 1792. [ERA]

TINTO, JOHN, son of William Tinto a grocer, was apprenticed to Alexander Steel, a merchant in Edinburgh, for five years, on 10 September 1795. [ERA]

TOD, ALEXANDER, a merchant in Philadelphia, Pennsylvania, brother and heir of Helen Tod, widow of John Stewart, a merchant in Edinburgh, in 1790. [NRS.S/H]

TODD, ALEXANDER, a lath-splitter, Junction Road, Leith, in 1849. [POD]

TOD, GEORGE, eldest son of George Tod a shipmaster in Leith, settled in Jamaica around 1778, a planter in St Thomas-in-the-East, died there in February 1808. [SM.71.158]

TOD, or TODDIE, or KIDD, JANET, in Edinburgh, heir to Lindsay Tod or Toddie, a cotton planter in America, in 1833. [NRS.S/H]

TORRANCE, AGNES, in Edinburgh, niece and heir of Andrew Jackson in USA, IN 1854. [NRS.S/H]

TOUGH, JOHN, a painter, was admitted as a burgess of Edinburgh on 2 September 1809 by right of his father George Tough a bellhanger burgess. [EBR]

TOWER, ALEXANDER, born 1801, died in Paris, France, on 3 August 1866, buried in Montmartre, husband of Eliza H. Dewhurst, born 16 September 1811, died on 22 November 1846. [St Cuthbert's gravestone, Edinburgh]

TROTTER, J., teacher of book-keeping, 10 North St David Street, Edinburgh, 1849. [POD]

TROTTER, THOMAS, son of William Trotter in Edinburgh, a Lieutenant of the Royal Artillery, died at Idanho Novo, Portugal, on 30 December 1812. [SM.75.238]

TROTTER, THOMAS, born in Leith, a stone mason, died in Halifax, Nova Scotia, on 6 October 1831. [Acadian Recorder. 15.10.1831]

TRUEFITT, W., a hairdresser and perfumer, 57 Princes Street, Edinburgh, 1849. [POD]

TULLIS, R., a wholesale stationer and paper maker, 14 St James Square, Edinburgh, 1849. [POD]

TULLOCH, ROBERT, of Golden Square, Edinburgh, married Mary Joanna Grant, only daughter of William Grant in Demerara, in Edinburgh in 1811. [SM.73.398]

TULLOCH, ROBERT, son of Dr James Tulloch a physician in Jamaica, was apprenticed to William Brown, a surgeon apothecary in Edinburgh for five years on 28 November 1790. [ERA]; a surgeon who died in Jamaica in 1812. [EA.5116.13]

TULLY, JOHN, a lodging house keeper in Edinburgh, versus his wife Agnes Steel, a Process of Divorces in 1827. [NRS.CC8.6.162]

TURNBULL, ALEXANDER, and his wife, Christian Thomson, [who died 19 January 1880], in Leith, parents of George Matheson Turnbull, a banker at Mount Gambier, South Australia. [NRS.S/H]

TURNBULL, ANDREW, born 1818, a printer from Edinburgh, who died in New York on 15 May 1876. [EC.28605][S.10256]; his eldest daughter Eliza Kincaid Monteith Turnbull, married William M. Connell, at 879 Broadway, New York, on 23 January 1868. [S.7656]

TURNBULL, GEORGE MATHESON, a banker in Mount Gambier, South Australia, son and heir of Christian Thomson, widow of

Alexander Turnbull, in Leith, who died on 19 January 1880. [NRS.S/H]

TURNBULL, JOHN, a merchant from Edinburgh, married Charlotte Evivitt, youngest daughter of Major Evivitt, in Kingston, Ontario, on 20 July 1821. [SM] [BM.10.358]

TURNBULL, ROBERT, son of John Turnbull a merchant, was apprenticed to John Murray, a baker in Edinburgh, for five years, on 12 December 1799. [ERA]

TURNER, CATHARINE AITKEN, daughter of Keith Turner of Turnerhall, married John George MacTavish of the Hudson Bay Company in Edinburgh on 22 February 1830. [BM.27.964]

TURNER, HENRY CASTLE, a printer in Canada, cousin and heir of James Castle, a goldsmith and jeweller in Edinburgh, who died on 26 May 1867. [NRS.S/H]

TURNER, MARY, versus her husband Robert Bamborough, a vintner in Leith, a Process of Divorce in 1796. [NRS.CC8.5.24]

TWEEDIE, ISABELLA, third daughter of Alexander Tweedie, a merchant in Edinburgh, married Thomas Thomson, a merchant from Louisiana, at Gayfield Square, Edinburgh, on 20 October 1824. [BM.16.614]

TWEEDIE, JANET, second daughter of Alexander Tweedie, a merchant in Edinburgh, married William Finch, a merchant from Louisiana, at Gayfield Square, Edinburgh, on 20 October 1824. [BM.16.615]

TWEEDIE, WILLIAM SIMPSON, fourth son of Alexander Tweedie a merchant in Edinburgh, died in Kingston, Jamaica, in January 1827. [S.755.216]

URE, JAMES, the Customs Controller in Leith, [1770-1848], husband of Margaret Innes, were parents of James Masterton Ure, who died in Murni Delice, Grenada on 20 September 1827. [Edinburgh, St Cuthbert's gravestone] [BM.23.270]

URQUHART, W., a plumber and gasfitter, 48 Canongate, Edinburgh, 1849. [POD]

USHER, A., wine and spirit merchant, 22 West Nicolson Street, Edinburgh, 1849. [POD]

UTRECHT, J. H., tailor, 72 George Street, Edinburgh, 1849. [POD]

VALLANCE, EUPHEMIA, versus her husband George Jeffrey a butcher in Edinburgh, a Process of Divorce in 1828. [NRS.CC8.6.155]

VALLANCE, JAMES, mate of the Jason of Leith, testament, 1802, Comm. Edinburgh. [NRS]

VALLANCE, WILLIAM, son of William Vallance and Elizabeth ...... his wife, was born on 27 March 1798, and baptised in the church of St John the Evangelist in Edinburgh on 5 April 1798. [NRS.CH12.3.26.2]

VALLANCE, WILLIAM, a baker at 18 Dean Street, Edinburgh, in 1849. [POD]

VAN CLEEK, ELIZABETH, widow of John Burt in New York, appointed Robert Burt, a physician in Edinburgh as her attorney, in 1817, deed refers to Catherine Burt, wife of Thomas Wilson, and Ann Burt, daughters and heirs of said John Burt. [NRS.RD5.177.575]

VARRAS, Mrs JACOBA HELENA, in Edinburgh, relict of Dr John Craigie of the East India Company, died on 16 January 1837, inventory 1837. [NRS]

VASS, MARIA CORNELIA, youngest daughter of Edward Brooke Vass in Florida, died at Greenhill Gardens, Edinburgh on 13 February 1854. [EEC.22543]

VEDDER, MAGNUS, an old clothes dealer in Steven Law's Close, Edinburgh, was accused of theft in 1815. [NRS.AD14.15.33]

VEITCH, CATHARINE, wife of William Grinton, a draper from Edinburgh then in North America, sister and heir of John Veitch, a merchant in Edinburgh, in 1862; also, heir to her brother James Veitch in Canada, who died on 9 September 1832 [NRS.S/H]

VEITCH, HUGH, elder of South Leith parish in 1825. [SLR]; town clerk Leith, a petitioner in 1828. [SLR]

VEITCH, THOMAS, a mason from Edinburgh, father of James Veitch, born 1869, and died in Hermitage, Pennsylvania, on 6 November 1871. [S.8838]

VERNON, J. E., born 1822, from Edinburgh, died in Dunedin, Otago, New Zealand, on 3 January 1899. [S.17359]

WADDELL, JAMES, in Kingston, Jamaica, heir to his sister Katherine Waddell in Edinburgh, in 1818. [NRS.S/H]

WAITS, DAVID, a merchant in Leith, was admitted as a burgess and guildsbrother of Edinburgh on 2 August 1815. [EBR]

WALDIE, JAMES, merchant,9 Stead's Place, Edinburgh, 1849. [POD]

WALKER, ALEXANDER, from Edinburgh, died in Charleston, South Carolina, probate 10 October 1792, S.C.

WALKER, ALEXANDER GORDON, in Logan County, America, grandson and heir of William Gibb the younger in Edinburgh, who died on 3 May 1829.; also, heir to his father James Walker in Edinburgh, in 1853. [NRS.S/H] [NRS.S/H]

WALKER, EMILIA, daughter of Alexander Walker in Queen Street, Edinburgh, wife of Edward Maxwell of the Bengal Civil Service, died aboard the Balcarres, an East Indiaman, on 26 July 1822. [SM.36.383]

WALKER, JAMES, a merchant in Leith, later Customs Collector in the Bahamas, dead by 1853, father of Agnes Elizabeth Walker and John Geddes Walker. [NRS.S/H]

WALKER, JOHN, son of John Walker a porter, was apprenticed to John Wood, a bookseller in Edinburgh, for six years, on 25 February 1790. [ERA]

WALKER, Major JOHN GEDDES, of the Royal Artillery, brother and heir of Agnes Walker, daughter and Customs Collector in Leith, later in the Bahamas, in 1853. [NRS.S/H]

WALKER, JOHN M., in Leith, father of Agnes Jane Walker, wife of Ninian Davidson, died in Quebec on 16 September 1874. [EC.28068]

WALKER, MAGDALENE HAY, in Edinburgh, sister and heir of Agnes Walker, daughter and Customs Collector in Leith, later in the Bahamas, in 1853. [NRS.S/H]

WALKER, THOMAS, born in Edinburgh, was naturalised in Charleston, South Carolina, on 20 September 1796. [NARA.M1183.1]

WALKER, THOMAS C., a commission agent and merchant in Edinburgh, a sederunt book in 1838, with debtors in Savannah, Georgia. [NRS.CS96.2361]

WALKER, WILLIAM, [1814-1893], and his wife Margaret Gray, [1815-1878], parents of James Gray Walker, born 1851, died in San Francisco, California, on 17 August 1891. [Grange gravestone, Edinburgh]

WALLACE, JOHN, in Leith, father of James Wallace, born 1852, died in Honolulu, Sandwich Islands, on 15 December 1897. [S.17035]

WALLACE, ..., a merchant, from Leith, in America in 1800. [NRS.CS17.1.18/416]

WALTERS, CATHERINE, born 1764 in Edinburgh, died in Savanna, Georgia, on 22 September 1808. [Savanna Death Register]

WARDEN, WILLIAM, son of John Warden a journeyman smith, was apprenticed to William Richardson, a locksmith in Edinburgh, for six years, on 12 April 1792. [ERA]

WARDLAW, WILLIAM, born 1824, a Lieutenant aboard HMS Racer, who was killed on the River Plate, Argentina, in 1846. [Dean gravestone, Edinburgh]

WARDROPE, DAVID, born in Edinburgh, a mariner who was naturalised in Charleston, South Carolina, on 2 July 1804. [NARA.M1183.1]

WARDROPE, JOHN, second son of David Wardrope a merchant in Edinburgh, a merchant who died in Portsmouth, New Hampshire, on 30 October 1804. [SM.67.74]

WARDROPE, MARGARET, third daughter of David Wardrope a surgeon in Edinburgh, wife of John Greenway of Belfast Plantation, died at Roseau, Dominica, on 6 May 1811. [DPCA][St Cuthbert's gravestone, Edinburgh] [SM.73.6371]

WATERSTON, GEORGE, a chandler, was admitted as a burgess of Edinburgh on 8 April 1816. [EBR];S wax chandler, 20 Hanover Street, Edinburgh, 1849. [POD]

WATSON, GEORGE, master of the Rothiemurchus of Leith from Leith bound for Quebec in 1817 and in 1818. [NRS.E504.22.76/80]

WATSON, JOHN, son of Captain Andrew Watson a merchant in Kingston, Jamaica, was admitted as a burgess of Edinburgh in 1792. [EBR]

WATSON, JOHN, jr., a merchant in Leith, married Isabella Walker Bolton, only child of Thomas Bolton a surgeon in Jamaica, in Green Park on 5 July 1827. [EA.6638.439]

WATSON, GEORGE, a portrait painter in Edinburgh, was admitted as a Member of the Academy of Arts in Charleston, South Carolina, in 1821. [EEC.17252]

WATSON, THOMAS B., an elder of South Leith parish on 1 October 1843. [SLR]

WATT, EDWARD LINDSAY, MD, in Jamaica, died in Edinburgh on 6 May 1812. [DPCA.877]

WATT, GEORGE, son of James Watt a mason in Bristo Street, Edinburgh, was apprenticed to John Porteous, a barber in Edinburgh, for six years, on 5 October 1797. [ERA]

WATT, JAMES, son of David Watt a miller in Stockbridge, was apprenticed to Alexander Swinton, a bookbinder in Edinburgh, for six years, on 11 May 1797. [ERA]

WATT, JAMES, born 1806 in Brechin, a wine merchant in Leith and Provost there, died in December 1881. [South Leith church window]

WATT, MARY, second daughter of John Watt, married Andrew Anderson, MD, eldest son of James Anderson in Devoespoint, New York, in Dunsmore Lodge, Corstorphine, Edinburgh, on 30 August 1816. [DPCA.736]

WATT, ROBERT, from Jamaica, graduated MD from Edinburgh University in 1803. [EMG.34]

WATT, WILLIAM, son of John Watt a brewer at the Water of Leith, was apprenticed for five years on 29 November 1799. [ERA]

WAUGH, PETER, son of Thomas Waugh a merchant in Leith, died in Jamaica in May 1807. [SM.69.718]

WEBSTER, Dr CHARLES, minister of St Paul's, Edinburgh, husband of ..... Graham of Balgowan, a chaplain to the troops in the West Indies, died on St Vincent in 1795. [JSC.89]

WEBSTER, DAVID, born 1810, a merchant in Leith, died in Montrose, Angus, on 4 January 1840. [Montrose gravestone]

WEBSTER, GEORGE, born 15 October 1744 in Edinburgh, son of Reverend Alexander Webster and his wife Mary Erskine, a civil paymaster in the Service of the East India Company, died in Bengal, India, in July 1794. [F.1.120]

WEDELL, ALEXANDER, a cart and plough wright in the Canongait, versus his wife Mary Banks, a Process of Divorce in 1812. [NRS.CC8.6.96]

WEDDELL, JAMES, a grocer, was admitted as a burgess of Edinburgh on 21 April 1829, by right of his father James Weddell a confectioner burgess. [EBR]

WEDDELL, THOMAS, a hosier and glover, 45 South Bridge, Edinburgh, in 1849. [POD]

WEIR, ANDREW, a candlemaker in Edinburgh, versus his wife Janet Kettle, a Process of Divorce in 1811. [NRS.CC8.5.32]

WEIR, JAMES, elder of South Leith parish in 1825. [SLR]

WEIR, MARGARET, wife of James Hindman, a plasterer in New York, daughter and heir of Robert Weir in Edinburgh, a Captain in the Service of the East India Company, who died on 20 November 1851. [NRS.S/H]

WEIR, SAMUEL, a silversmith, 13 Chalmer's Close, Edinburgh, 1849. [POD]

WEIR, THOMAS HERIOT, deacon of South Leith parish in 1825. [SLR]; a baker in Leith, a petitioner in 1828. [SLR]

WELLS, ANDREW, from Edinburgh, died in Monte Video, Uruguay, on 25 March 1867. [S.7413]

WELLSTOOD, MARY, born 1818, eldest daughter of James Wellstood in Edinburgh, died in Vineland, New Jersey, on 30 November 1874. [S.9804]

WELSH, ELEANOR, second daughter of Dominick Welsh in Jamaica, married Stewart West, from Kingston, Jamaica, in Edinburgh on 9 June 1828. [EA.6735.383]; parents of a daughter born in Kingston, Jamaica, on 27 April 1829. [BM.26.410]

WELSH, JAMES, in St Kitts, heir to his father James Welsh, a postal worker in Edinburgh, who died on 10 May 1850, and heir to his mother Jane Begbie, widow of James Welsh, who died on 27 April 1852. [NRS.S/H]

WELSH, WILLIAM, in Edinburgh, father of Henrietta Welsh, born 1863, died in Durban, Natal, South Africa. On 27 March 1885. [S.13045]

WEMYSS, A. S, a trunk and portmanteau maker, 8 South St Andrew Street, Edinburgh, 1849. [POD]

WEMYSS, DAVID, son of George Wemyss a butcher in the Canongait, was apprenticed to William Watson, a wright in Edinburgh for six years, on 5 August 1790. [ERA]

WEST, WILLIAM, Captain of the Corps of Edinburgh Volunteers, was admitted as a burgess and guildsbrother of Edinburgh on 10 September 1790. [EBR]

WHARTON, GEORGE, a scale, beam, and steelyard maker, 59 Leith Wynd, Edinburgh, 1849. [POD]

WHYTE, AGNES BRYSON, born 1824, daughter of Robert Whyte, a merchant, and his wife Agnes Bryson, wife of James Sneddon a civil engineer in Savannah, Georgia, died on 2 December 1854. [Greyfriars gravestone, Edinburgh]

WHITE, ADAM, a shipmaster in Leith, testament, 1803, Comm. Edinburgh. [NRS]

WHITE, ADAM, elder of South Leith parish in 1825. [SLR]; a merchant in Leith, a petitioner in 1828; an elder on 1 October 1843. [SLR]

WHITE, ADAM, born 1799, Lieutenant Colonel of the 59th Regiment of Bengal Native Infantry, was killed in action in Upper Assam on 18 January 1839. [South Leith gravestone]

WHITE, DOMINICK, born 1789 in County Monaghan, Ireland, a labourer in Plainstone Close, Edinburgh, was accused of theft in 1849. [NRS.AD14.49.118]

WHITE, GEORGE, born 1807 in Edinburgh, was naturalised in Charleston, South Carolina, on 3 August 1831. [NARA.M1183.1]

WHYTE, JAMES, a surgeon in the Service of the East India Company, died in Edinburgh on 27 January 1826, inventory 1827. [NRS]

WHYTE, JAMES, and WILLIAM, WHYTE, merchants in Leith, sederunt book in 1828, creditors in Virginia and New York. [NRS.CS96.443]

WHITE, JOHN, born 1790 in Edinburgh, a stonecutter in Charleston, South Carolina, was naturalised there on 10 October 1826. [NARA.M1183.1]

WHITE, JOHN, in Leith, applied to settle in Canada on 1 March 1815. [NRS.RH9]

WHITE, JOHN JARVIS, master of the Vigilant of Leith, testament, 1826, Comm. Edinburgh. [NRS]

WHITE, WILLIAM, a chairmaker in Rose Street, Edinburgh, was admitted as a burgess of Edinburgh on 12 April 1841 by right of his wife Isabella Watson, daughter of Thomas Watson, a wright burgess. [EBR]

WHYTE, WILLIAM, son of Robert Whyte, [1778-1851], a merchant, and his wife Agnes Bryson, [1787-1847], died in Detroit, Michigan, on 18 September 1892. [Greyfriars gravestone, Edinburgh]

WHITEHEAD, ELIZABETH, from Edinburgh, wife of Reverend Daniel Anderson a missionary, died in Brock, Canada West, on 5 November 1859. [CM.21617]

WHITELAW, DAVID, a brewer in Portsburgh, was admitted as a burgess of Edinburgh on 20 May 1807, by right of his wife Janet Scott, daughter of William Scott a pewterer burgess. [EBR]

WHITSON, ROBERT, an elder of South Leith parish on 1 October 1843. [SLR]

WHITSON, ..., son of Archibald Whitson from Edinburgh, died in Calleo, Peru, on 18 June 1870. [S.8422]

WIGHAM, J., a shawl manufacturer, 51 Nicolson Street, Edinburgh, 1849. [POD]

WIGHT, ANDREW, a farmer in Madison County, Missouri, nephew and heir of Beatrice Wight in Edinburgh, in 1831. [NRS.S/H]

WIGHT, DAVID, son of Claude Wight and former apprentice to Robert Annan, now a merchant and the Swedish Consul in Leith, was admitted as a burgess and guilds-brother of Edinburgh on 4 December 1804. [EBR]

WIGHT, WILLIAM, late from Jamaica, died in Edinburgh on 28 March 1817. [S.I.11]

WIGHTMAN, W., a contractor, Trinity Crescent, Edinburgh, 1849. [POD]

WIGHTON, GEORGE DICKSON, a clerk in Colorado, son and heir of William Wighton, a watchmaker in Edinburgh, who died on 7 November 1866. [NRS.S/H]

WILKIE, JOHN, a seaman of the Hibernia of Leith, was drowned in its shipwreck, when bound from St John, New Brunswick, to Liverpool, on 19 January 1810. [NBRG]

WILKIESON, ANTHONY, a gunsmith, was admitted as a burgess of Edinburgh on 1 September 1796 by right of his wife Margaret Gardner, daughter of William Gardner a dyster burgess. [EBR]

WILLIAMS, JOHN, a pocketbook and jewel case manufacturer, was admitted as a burgess of Edinburgh on 31 January 1831. [EBR]

WILLIAMSON, ALEXANDER, a surgeon from Edinburgh, died on Montserrat on 29 August 1829. [BM.27.134]

WILLIAMSON, BENJAMIN, eldest son of Captain Williamson of 5 Raeburn Place, Edinburgh, died in New Orleans, Luisiana, in April 1841. [EEC.20224]

WILLIAMSON, CHARLES, born 1757 in Edinburgh, an officer of the British Army, later emigrated to America in 1790, an agent for the Pultenet Estate in western New York State from 1790 to 1800, founder of Bath, N.Y., died in New Orleans, Louisiana, in September 1808. [SSA]

WILLIAMSON, CHARLES, a metal merchant, 79 St Andrew Street, Leith, 1849. [POD]

WILLIAMSON, F., a parchment maker, Bonnington Bridge, Edinburgh, 1849. [POD]

WILLIAMSON, GEORGE, a clerk in Edinburgh, heir to his grand-uncle Alexander Naughton in Tobago, who died in 1829. [NRS.S/H]

WILLIAMSON, JAMES, born 13 March 1810 in Edinburgh, a metal broker in New York from 1837 to his death on 23 January 1872. [ANY]

WILLIAMSON, THOMAS, born 1758 in Edinburgh, a gentleman who married Matilda …., emigrated via Greenock to New York, was naturalised in New York on 16 November 1818. [NARA]

WILLIAMSON, WILLIAM, a saddler in Edinburgh, was admitted as a burgess of Dunfermline on 27 June 1794. [DM]

WILLIAMSON and GAVIN, rope and sail makers and tenants in the Bush, Leith, in 1811. [LD]

WILLOX, ALEXANDER, in High Street, Leith, a former gunner of the Royal Artillery, applied to emigrate to Canada in 1819. [TNA.CO384.5.327]

WILSON, ADAM, a writer in Edinburgh, son of John Wilson a mason burgess of Dunfermline, was admitted as a burgess of Dunfermline on 28 October 1791. [DM]

WILSON, ALEXANDER, in New York, son and heir of William Wilson, a mason in Edinburgh, in 1821. [NRS.S/H]

WILSON, ANDREW, born 1806 in Edinburgh, son of Andrew Wilson, died in Toronto, Canada, on 18 October 1864. [GM.ns.3.1.141]

WILSON, ANDREW, from Leith, died in Valparaiso, Chile, in 1863. [S.2456]

WILSON, CHARLES, [1842-1866], father of Daniel Wilson, born 1866, died in Detroit, Michigan, on 5 July 1898. [Dean gravestone, Edinburgh]

WILSON, DANIEL, a Doctor in Law in Toronto University, nephew of Peter Wilson in Edinburgh, who died on 26 January 1864. [NRS.S/H]

WILSON, FRANCIS, from Edinburgh, an innkeeper in Halifax, Nova Scotia, settled in Tatamagouche, NS, in 1817. [HT]

WILSON, FLETCHER, on Auchenleck's Brae, Newhaven, the victim of theft in 1849. [NRS.AC14.49.109]

WILSON, Dr GEORGE, in Stonecleugh, late of Edinburgh, married Marianne Banister, daughter of John Banister, late Congressman, and niece of Theororic Baine a Member of Congress for Virginia, on 19 March 1789. [SM.51.412[; formerly a physician in Petersburg, Virginia, died in London on 13 October 1799. [EA.1738.271]

WILSON, GEORGE, born 1803 in Edinburgh, a pilot in Charleston, South Carolina, was naturalised there on 19 August 1826. [NARA.M1183.1]

WILSON, JAMES, at the College of William and Mary in Virginia, brother and heir of Mary Wilson, wife of Robert Smith a tailor in Leith, in 1792. [NRS.S/H]

WILSON, JAMES, born 1774 in Leith, son of James Wilson a maltster in Leith, a merchant in Charleston, South Carolina, naturalised there on 13 July 1807, died in Crieff, Perthshire, on 27 December 1823. [EA][NARA.M1183.1]

WILSON, JANE BROWN, only daughter of John Wilson, an advocate in Edinburgh, married Reverend Louis Cochet, a minister of the French Reformed Church, a missionary to the Basutos, in Cape Town, Cape of Good Hope, South Africa, on 3 November 1847. [EEC.21608][SG.1685]

WILSON, JOHN, born 1767 in Leith, a cartman who emigrated via Portsmouth to USA, was naturalised in New York on 31 March 1821. [NARA]

WILSON, JOHN, master of the Leopold of Leith bound from Leith to Halifax, Nova Scotia, and Quebec in 1819. [NRS.E504.22.85]

WILSON, JOHN, born 1800 in Edinburgh, a vocalist, died in Quebec on 8 July 1849. [GM.ns.32.547][Dean gravestone, Edinburgh]

WILSON, JOHN, born 1838, son of James Wilson in Edinburgh, died aboard HMS Camelon in Valparaiso, Chile, on 15 November 1870. [S.8558]

WILSON, PATRICK, teacher of English and Geography, High School of Leith, Whitehouse, Duke Street, Edinburgh, 1849. [POD]

WILSON, Captain ROBERT, born in 1850, died in Rio de Janeiro, Brazil, on 7 April 1894. [Dean gravestone, Edinburgh]

WILSON, THOMAS, born 1758 in Edinburgh, was naturalised in New York on 16 November 1818. [NY Court of Common Pleas Records]

WILSON, WALTER, his wife, and son, from Edinburgh, died in Hamilton, Canada West, in 1854. [S.6.9.1854]

WILSON, WILLIAM, son of John Wilson a wright in Portsburgh, was apprenticed to James Donaldson, a printer in Edinburgh, for seven years, on 27 April 1797. [ERA]

WILSON, WILLIAM, a smith in Edinburgh, versus his wife Christian Gemmel or Gamble, a Process of Divorce in 1798. [NRS.CC8.5.24]

WILSON, WILLIAM, son of Thomas Wilson a writer in Edinburgh, died in Surinam on 6 August 1812. [SM.7.886]

WILSON, WILLIAM, born 1788 in Edinburgh, a butcher in Charleston, South Carolina, naturalised there on 23 October 1813. [NARA.M1183.1]

WILSON, WILLIAM, born 1811, second son of James Wilson, a Member of the Legislative Council of Queensland, Australia, died 3 March 1887, buried in Kensal Green Cemetery in London. [St Cuthbert's gravestone, Edinburgh]

WINGRAVE, WILLIAM MEARNS, in Bonn, Germany, son and heir of Mathew Wingrove in Kirkbank, Edinburgh, who died on 23 November 1848. [NRS.S/H]

WINKWORTH, JAMES, a bookbinder, was admitted as a burgess of Edinburgh on 31 March 1825. [EBR]

WINT, THOMAS KINCAID, MD, formerly a medical student in Edinburgh, died in Spanish Town, Jamaica, on 3 November 1812. [EA.5120.13]

WINTON, GEORGE, a mason in Edinburgh, married Violet Robertson in April 1808, Process of Divorce, in January 1827. [NRS.CC8.6.153]

WINTOUR, JOHN MAITLAND, a painter, was admitted as a burgess of Edinburgh on 6 August 1822 by right of his father Alexander Mitchelson Wintour a painter burgess. [EBR]

WISHART, JAMES, a ship broker and wharfinger, a tenant in the Bush, Leith, in 1811. [LD]

WISHART, JOHN, born 1801, a shipmaster in Leith, died in Macao, China, on 2 November 1843. [North Leith gravestone]

WISHART, Reverend THOMAS, born 9 June 1809, died in St John, New Brunswick, on 12 January 1853. [Greyfriars gravestone, Edinburgh]

WISHART, PHILADELPHIA ANNE, born 13 February 1814, wife of William MacNider MD in Montreal, Quebec, died on 29 October 1890. [Greyfriars gravestone, Edinburgh]

WODROP, JOHN, born 8 July 1756 in Edinburgh, a merchant in Charleston, South Carolina, died there on 31 July 1828. [St Michael's gravestone, Charleston]

WOOD, Dr ANDREW, in Ipswich, England, heir to his unce Andrew Baird, a bookseller in Edinburgh, later in Jamaica, in 1827. [NRS.S/H]

WOOD, GEORGE, eldest son of Lord Wood in Edinburgh, married Emma Henry, eldest daughter of Barnard Henry in Philadelphia, Pennsylvania, on 17 April 1845. [GM.ns24.72]; parents of a daughter born there on 11 September 1846. [W.VII.22]

WOOD, GEORGE, agent in Philadelphia, Pennsylvania, for the Royal Insurance Company, heir to his granduncle Sir Alexander Wood in Edinburgh, who died on 18 March 1847; also, heir to his father Alexander Wood of Woodcot, Midlothian, who died on 18 July 1864. [NRS.S/H]

WOOD, JAMES, born 14 March 1840, son of Reverend James Julius Wood and his wife Christian Inglis in New Greyfriars, Edinburgh, a banker in Sydney, New South Wales, Australia. [F.1.35]

WOOD, JANET, wife of John Gray Moxey, a baker in Philadelphia, Pennsylvania, daughter and heir of John Wood in Edinburgh, in 1853. [NRS.S/H]

WOOD, JOHN, a merchant in Leith, was admitted as a burgess and guildsbrother of Edinburgh on 17 December 1827, by right of his father Peter Wood, a merchant in Leith. [EBR]

WOOD, ROBERT WALKER, an engraver in Edinburgh, brother and heir of Thomas Wood in Magnolia, New Orleans, Louisiana, who died on 18 October 1857. [NRS.S/H]

WOOD, WILLIAM, a surgeon, was admitted as a burgess of Edinburgh on 6 September 1805, by right of his father Andrew Wood a surgeon burgess. [EBR]

WOOD, WILLIAM, CHRISTOPHER WOOD jr, and WILLIAM WOOD, merchants in Leith, versus James Lockie, a merchant in Dunbar, in 1830. [NRS.SC40.20.154.10]

WOOD, WILLIAM, a provision merchant in Edinburgh, son and heir of Margaret Clark, wife of Simon Wood in America, who died on 1 September 1849. [NRS.S/H]

WOODWARD, RUFUS, born 16 July 1793 in Torringford, Connecticut, graduated from Yale University in 1816, died in Edinburgh on 24 November 1823. [St Cuthbert's gravestone]

WORDSWORTH, SAMUEL, a horse dealer, was admitted as a burgess of Edinburgh by right of his wife Sarah Pool, daughter of Matthew Pool a vintner burgess, on 24 June 1808. [EBR]; a livery stable keeper, Nottingham Place, Edinburgh, in 1849. [POD]

WOTHERSPOON, WILLIAM, an accountant in Edinburgh, versus his wife Elizabeth Young, a Process of Divorce in 1817. [NRS.CC8.5.36]; , was admitted as a burgess and guildsbrother of Edinburgh, by right of his father John Wotherspoon a printer burgess, on 6 September 1810. [EBR]

WRIGHT, ALEXANDER MALCOLM, in New York, son and heir of Alexander Wright in Pilrig Street, Edinburgh, who died on 23 September 1866. [NRS.S/H]

WRIGHT, GEORGE, an upholsterer and cabinetmaker, was admitted as a burgess of Edinburgh on 15 January 1807. [EBR]

WRIGHT, WILLIAM, a dyer, was admitted as a burgess of Edinburgh on 27 May 1816. [EBR]

WRIGHT, WILLIAM, born 1735 in Crieff, late physician to the army in the West Indies, died in Edinburgh in 1819. [Grayfriars gravestone]

WRIGHT, WILLIAM SMITH, of Caracas, Venezuela, natural son of Colonel Robert Wright, late of the Royal Artillery, Leith Fort, 31 July 1829. [NRS.PS3.15/20]

WYBAR, JAMES, a painter in New York, son and heir of George Wybar, a sawyer in Edinburgh, in 1857. [NRS.S/H]

WYLIE, ALEXANDER, an iron and seed merchant in Candlemaker Row, was admitted as a burgess of Edinburgh on 21 May 1840. [EBR]

WYLLIE, JAMES, a soldier of C Company of the 1st Michigan Cavalry, died in the American Civil War, 1861-1865. [Old Calton gravestone, Edinburgh]

YEAMAN, JAMES, son of Alexander Yeaman, a wheelwright and turner, was apprenticed to George Skelton a clock and watchmaker in Edinburgh, for seven years on 23 June 1791. [ERA]

YOUNG, ALEXANDER, a builder in Edinburgh, emigrated to America in 1795 to join his son there. [NRS.GD51]

YOUNG, ALEXANDER, a shipmaster in Leith, testament, 1817, Comm. Edinburgh. [NRS.CC8.8.143.144]

YOUNG, ALEXANDER, a Writer to the Signet in Edinburgh, the recipient of a letter from Captain Frederick Marryat, the author, in 1840. [NRS.GD214.747.20]

YOUNG, HELEN CLARKE, in America, daughter and heir of James Young in Lilliesleaf, Roxburghshire, later in Edinburgh, in 1848. [NRS.S/H]

YOUNG, JAMES, a brewer in Leith, father of Thomas Young who died in Jamaica on 24 October 1798. [AJ.2661]

YOUNG, JAMES, from Edinburgh, settled in Columbia, South Carolina, was naturalised in S.C. on 5 December 1806. [NARA.M1183.1]

YOUNG, JOHN, a surgeon, as husband of Isobel McKenzie, daughter of Kenneth McKenzie a druggist burgess, was admitted as a burgess and guildsbrother of Edinburgh on 24 June 1808. [EBR]

YOUNG, JOHN, jr., a merchant, married Jemima Stewart Steven, eldest daughter of William Steven of Edinburgh, in Hamilton, Upper Canada, on 5 March 1844. [W.V.454]

YOUNG, JOHN, born 1789, died in Calcutta, India, on 13 September 1836. [North Leith gravestone]

YOUNG, JOHN LAWSON, in Melbourne, Victoria, Australia, son and heir of David Young, an Excise officer in Edinburgh who died o 10 December 1872. [NRS.S/H]

YOUNG, MATTHEW, son of George Young a brewer in Fisherrow, remained apprenticed to William Young a baker for five years, on 10 May 1792. [ERA]

YOUNG, RICHARD, a brewer, died in 1840, husband of Isabella Liddel Cramond, died 1865. [Grayfriars gravestone]

YOUNG, THOMAS, second son of James Young a brewer in Leith, died in Jamaica on 24 October 1798. [AJ.2661]

YOUNG, THOMAS, a solicitor in Hobart, Tasmania, nephew and heir of Annabella Fullerton Young in Edinburgh in 1835. [NRS.S/H]

YOUNG, THOMAS, a merchant in Leith, was admitted as a burgess and guildsbrother of Edinburgh on 26 July 1838. [EBR]

YOUNG, WILLIAM, a Writer to the Signet, married Agnes Gerard, daughter of James Gerard of Whitehaugh, in Edinburgh on 21 January 1820. [SM.85]

YOUNG, WILLIAM, a cutler, son of Archibald Young a cutler, was admitted as a burgess of Edinburgh on 28 January 1829. [EBR]

YOUNG, WILLIAM, a colour manufacturer in Silverfield, Leith, 1849. [POD]

YOUNG, ..., master of the whaler Raith of Leith, from Leith via Lerwick to Greenland in March 1786. [AJ.1994]; was captured off Shetland, on the return voyage from Greenland, by a French privateer, and taken to Dunkirk in 1794. [PL.296]

YOUNGER, ARCHIBALD CAMPBELL, a brewer, was admitted as a burgess and guildsbrother of Edinburgh on 17 September 1807. [EBR]

YULE, JAMES, a baker, son of John Yule a baker burgess, was admitted as a burgess of Edinburgh on 16 March 1812. [EBR]

YULE, WILLIAM, a baker, son of John Yule a baker burgess, was admitted as a burgess of Edinburgh on 11 May 1797. [EBR]

ZIEGLER, JOHN, a cloth merchant, son of John Ziegler a silversmith, was admitted as a burgess of Edinburgh on 3 June 1825. [EBR]

REFERENCES

AJ   Aberdeen Journal, series

ANY   St Andrew's Society of New York

AP   St Andrew's Society of Philadelphia

BA   Officers of the Bengal Army

BM   Blackwood's Magazine, series

BPP   British Parliamentary Papers

CM   Caledonian Mercury, series

CMSA   Colonial Museum and Savannah Advertiser, series

DCB   Directory of Canadian Biography

DPCA   Dundee, Perth, & Cupar Advertiser, series

EA   Edinburgh Advertiser, series

EAR   Edinburgh Academy Register

EBR   Edinburgh Burgess Roll

EC   Edinburgh Courant, series

ECA   Edinburgh City Archives

EEC   Edinburgh Evening Courant, series

EMA Emigrant Ministers to America, 1690-1811

EMG Edinburgh Medical Graduates

EMR Edinburgh Marriage Register

ERA Edinburgh Register of Apprentices

FH Fife Herald, series

FPA Fulham Papers, American

GC Glasgow Courier, series

GH Glasgow Herald, series

GM Gentleman's Magazine, series

HBRS Hudson Bay Record Society

IC Inverness Courier, series

IJ Inverness Journal, series

JSC A Jacobite Stronghold of the Church

LCL Leith Commercial Lists, series

MHS A Maritime History of Scotland, 1650-1790.

NARA National Archives Records Administration, Washington, DC

NBC New Brunswick Courier, series

NBRG New Brunswick Royal Gazette, series

NCA North Carolina Archives, Raleigh

NEHGS New England Historic Genealogical Society, Boston

NJSA New Jersey State Archives, Trenton

NRS National Records of Scotland, Edinburgh

OC Old Churches, Ministers, and Families of Virginia

OEC Book of the Old Edinburgh Club, series

PANS Public Archives, New Brunswick

PAPEI Public Archives, Prince Edward Island

PCC Prerogative Court of Canterbury

PL The Port of Leith

POD Post Office Directory, series

PRONI Public Record Office of Northern Ireland, Belfast

QM Quebec Mercury

RGS Register of the Great Seal of Scotland

S The Scotsman, series

SAB Bergen, Norway, Archives

SBR Stirling Burgess Roll

SC Southern Chronicle, series

SCGaz South Carolina Gazette, series

SCS Scots Charitable Society, Boston

SG Scottish Guardian, series

SHS Scottish History Society

S/H Services of Heirs

SLIM South Leith Irregular Marriages

SLR South Leith parish register

SM Scots Magazine, series

SRP   Scots on the River Plate

SRS   Scottish Record Society

SSA Scots and Scots Descendants in America, [NY.1917]

THD   Trinity House Declarations

TNA The National Archives of the UK, Kew

VJ Virginia Journal, series

W Witness, series

WMC William Melrose in China, 1845-1855, [Edinburgh, 1973]

ZA Zealand Archives, Rotterdam

www.ingramcontent.com/pod-product-compliance
Lightning Source LLC
Chambersburg PA
CBHW052100230426
43662CB00036B/1712